THE CHURCH IN TRANSITION
REFORM IN THE CHURCH OF ENGLAND

THE REFORM SERIES

The
Church in Transition

REFORM IN THE CHURCH OF ENGLAND

DEWI MORGAN

Rector of the Church of St Bride, Fleet Street

1970

CHATTO & WINDUS
CHARLES KNIGHT
LONDON

Chatto & Windus Ltd.,
Charles Knight & Co. Ltd.
London

*

Clarke, Irwin & Co. Ltd.
Toronto

SBN 7011 1617 X (hardcover)
SBN 7011 1618 8 (paperback)

Printed in Great Britain by
R. and R. Clark Ltd.
Edinburgh

Contents

Declaration of Intent

To include a book on the Church of England in a series on the reform of our national institutions could appear to some to be an unprofitable exercise. To the cynic, this oldest of all our English entities (ante-dating even the word 'English') can seem beyond rehabilitation. Let its terminal illness be undisturbed, could well be his comment. The book would certainly not have been written had the author shared his sentiment. But those who understand and love this Church of England can also question the wisdom of such a book, for they know that *ecclesia semper reformanda* is of its essence. The Church, to be the Church, must always be in the throes of reformation.

A Declaration of Intent is therefore called for, if only to encourage the reader beyond page one.

This is not another of those books which attempt to capture in words both the deep mysteries of the inner life of the Church of England and also its patchwork outer structure which has grown through the perennial cobbling of ancient wineskins.

To attempt to pontificate on that structure would, at this moment, be folly indeed. For major changes are imminent. They have been argued at tedious length but even so none can prophesy just how they are going to work. These major changes will no doubt be followed by others. And if ever an author's aspirations that his words should be as true on the day they are read as on the day they are written be realised, then he will not be writing about the Church of England as we know it.

The philosophers have long bewildered themselves by contemplating the flight of an arrow. At any moment it must be totally existent in one place yet, since motion is its heart, it can never be wholly in one place. The metaphor may not seem wholly appropriate, for few people get the impression that the Church of England is shot from some powerful bow and goes hence unerringly to a target. Yet motion, process, change, is part of its essence. For it constantly seeks the God who is bigger than we thought and who ever remains bigger than we can think. Its inner life and thought must therefore ever be growing. And, no less, this Church of England knows itself to be incarnate in a human society where the changes of the centuries have exploded into the revolution of our day. From within and from without, the demand is to adapt to change.

It is traditional to be modern but the twentieth century calls for something more. Today there must be an utter flexibility which permits a response to unprecedented situations. Yet there is ultimately nothing new in this. The Church of England has always been in a process of response to the demand for adaptation. It seems to have realised something that the instinct of our language has enshrined: that the word 'becoming' means not only a process of changes but also a state of being agreeable, befitting, adorning. Such an idiom arrives not by accident but as a crystallisation of a deep feeling of the race. It is becoming that the Church of England should always be becoming.

This book pays relatively little attention to structures, then, because structures are impermanent, always open to improvement. But there is also another reason. Like the average car driver, people have little interest in what is under the bonnet of the Church of England. They want to know where the car is going. They try to check that it has enough spirit to ensure progress. Then they leave the deep mysteries of mechanics to those who like such things. The reaction of the public to the niceties of the structure of the body ecclesiastic or its canon laws or any other of the ingroup and very time-absorbing formulae is the sort of boredom which easily flares into irritation. This book tries not to irritate.

What, rather, it seeks to do is to offer a personal view of someone whose ordination is now many years since but who has enjoyed every one of them and hopes to enjoy at least a few more. Being a priest has proved an exuberant existence. Exuberance is surely something to be shared.

There is, too, a slightly odd element in my background. It cannot have happened often that the very first day when a man became *technically* a member of the Church of England was the day he was made Rector of a parish in the City of London. Until comparatively recently I felt able to view this Church of England as an outsider and there linger in my mind feelings that while very much its servant I still see it from the outside. I dare to believe that gives me some element of objectivity. Those few lines may be puzzling: if so, a soupçon of autobiography is called for.

Spiritually I have always been a part of what the Church of England stands for. But that did not make me one of its members. I was born into the Church in Wales disestablished and disendowed, baptised in that Church, grew up in it, was ordained in it and served as one of its priests until, unexpectedly, I found myself in London on the staff of the Society for the Propagation of the Gospel. An office in Westminster seemed emotionally (even though it was part of such a welcoming family) an alien place for a Welshman who had always been accustomed to hear 'those English' spoken of as foreign. Furthermore, that office, being the headquarters of England's oldest missionary-sending society, was more concerned with the life of the Church in the remoter ends of the earth than with the details which were debated in the Church Assembly or the Convocations across the road.

The consequence was the strengthening of my early conviction that while the specific vehicle of my membership, including my ordination, had been the Church in Wales, the roots really lay in the Church Universal. Added to that was the technicality that the nature of my work during those twelve years did not necessitate my being licensed in any diocese of the Church of England. I regarded myself as being on loan from Wales. I was indeed a priest of identical status with any priest in the Church of England. But the Church of England, while accepting my priesthood, had not formally authorised me to be responsible for any part of its work. That came only when, and with no small surprise, I found that I had become Rector of St Bride's.

For seven-eighths of my life I have not regarded myself as a member of the Church of England. Yet for approaching half my life I have been fairly intimately involved in its life. I have spent much time as an outsider looking in. As I have stood outside, my mental vantage point has ranged from Wales to Africa to India to the United States, across the world wherever the Anglican Communion has been sown. That Anglican Communion is in some senses the Church of England writ large. In others, and very important ones, it is something quite different, yet by those very differences providing a further insight into the Church of England.

One further factor remains to be mentioned. Fleet Street is as international a spot as any in the world. To be Rector of St Bride's is to share with John Wesley the thought that the world is my parish. Contantly in my daily pastoral work the emphasis falls on the world outside England. And no less does it fall on the world outside the Church. For while Fleet Street contains what I would regard as a remarkably high number of committed practising Christians, it is essentially a domain of the secular. To aim, day by day, to tell the world about the world is to enter the heart of secularity.

All of which is not intended in any way to be an *apologia*. Nor is it all related in order to prove that I have some unique point of view. It is merely that such a background seems relevant. And if one offers a book to a reader one must offer not only words but also the context in which they were written.

That context can most succinctly be expressed by admitting that the title for this book was at one stage going to be 'Beloved Exasperation'. That there are many times when I feel exasperated by this Church of England is undeniable. It shows such brilliant ingenuity in devising bushels big enough to obscure its candles. and it not infrequently has an air of lethargy which suggests that any reform possible today must inevitably be better if left to tomorrow. There is so much in this Church which justifies the remark 'Anglicanism is the worst form of religion – except for any other'.

The Church of England has done its share to prove that men cannot be trusted with the things of God lest they ruin them. But it has also done its share to prove that God insists in entrusting his things to men and there are times when they do not fail him. There is so much to love, so much, indeed, which compels love in this Church of England. And so there is the continuing dialogue between exasperation and fascination. And once more we are back at what must remain an unavoidable word when one considers this Church: process.

If the reader demands final, spelt out and irrefutable statements about the Church of England, he had best stop here. But if he wants to come along a personal way, we welcome him. He will find no efficient modern highway, cutting insensitively through hill and dale and leaving only the monotony of efficiency as he speeds to his goal. Rather we offer the way which began roughly when the Romans first come to Rye and English roads first snaked their way, reeling, rolling, drunken. It may appear like going to Birmingham by way of Beachy Head but it will also suggest a route for going to Paradise without leaving out Kensal Green.

I

Thinking

'A woman when she is in travail hath sorrow, because her hour is come: but as soon as she is delivered of the child, she remembereth no more the anguish, for joy that a man is born into the world.'

It was the dominical authority of that illustration, used by Jesus in a very solemn moment, that finally decided the shape of this book. Was it to begin with history? The argument was powerful, for without knowing its becoming it is hard to enter into the being of the Church of England. Yet this is a generation so conditioned by the contemporary revolution that it finds dallying with the past tedious. There is little time to look over your shoulder when you are hurtling forward into an unknown. And when that unknown is as exciting as our posterity's promises to be, there is little inclination for backward glances. This book will be incomplete if it has no room for history. Yet it is with the present as the ground of the future that we must first be concerned. What is past is God's, what is future is God's, what is present is both his and mine, so someone said. Accordingly Clio must wait until we have surveyed the landscape before we consult her about the road by which we arrived here.

27,658,000 people are baptised members of the Church of England according to the most recent statistics. Why?

An honest answer would be that the majority of them have such membership because their parents had it before them. They were born into this Church. To say that does not diminish this Church, for one could say the same thing about the majority of Roman Catholics or Muslims or any other religious allegiance. Yet it is more true of English Churchmen than of most, for the Church of England has become part of the English way of life – which results in hard-to-audit balance-sheets of profits and losses. For nineteen centuries or so this Church has been both active and passive in English history, moulding and being moulded, interacting with its environment as an organic part of the whole until neither sociologist nor theologian can tell where membership begins and ends. Any parson can speak of men who never go inside a church door yet they fiercely–and sincerely–protest their membership of the Church of England. Even the most careful probing leaves one assured of their deep conviction that they are telling the truth. But surely, it must be asked, someone is bound to know whether or not they are members? There must be some standard of judgement?

In the first place, the Church of England is not like some factory with a timeclock at its gate on which all must stamp their cards as they enter. Nor does it require of visiting strangers the production of any credentials before they approach its altars– though he would be a very untypical and casual parish priest who saw someone approach regularly without seeking to establish the closer contact which led to greater knowledge and consequent action. The basic instinct of the Church of England is to include rather than exclude, to write Welcome on its doormats rather than to make membership conditional upon rigorous examination.

Yet to say these things is to skate the real question: does the Church of England have any recognisable body of beliefs which includes some and excludes others? The immediate answer is quite unquestionably Yes. For the only way to become one of its members is by baptism and the service prescribed for that includes a number of propositions to which the baptismal candidate either personally or by the proxy of godparents must give firm assent before the sacrament can be administered. But an immediate answer can be misleading and especially in this context. For it involves squeezing an ocean of thought into the bucket of a sentence. Our Yes of a moment ago is misleading because it implies that there is some body of belief which is exclusively and characteristically the mark of the Church of England. There are many reasons why that is not the case. Among them is the fact that within the Church of England can be detected a legitimate range of belief and also the fact that there is no belief of the Church of England which cannot be found to be part of the belief of some other Church.

But first let us be positive and express, even though it be cursorily, what the Church of England asserts.

It asserts that there is one God and he is personal and has certain attributes. He has a will with which some things are consistent and others are not. He made everything and he wants men to share with him and respond to him.

Because men failed in this, God sent the pattern Man, Jesus Christ whose birth, life, death and resurrection showed men what God is really like and therefore what they are to strive to be like. This Jesus also opened up the possibility of men achieving this likeness because he created a new situation of relationship sustained by his strength. This situation is relevant to every human circumstance and all who will accept his conditions can freely enter into it and gain the dynamic it derives from him.

To perpetuate his work, Jesus promised men the companionship of his Spirit and he said that while this Spirit could and would work in all sorts of ways, his primary sphere of operations would be a Society which Jesus called into being and of which he would always remain Head. The inception of this Society, the Church, occurred very shortly after Jesus' earthly work was finally concluded and it has grown down the centuries and across the world. It has become known as the Holy (for while being in the world it is also set apart with God) Catholic (for it is universal) Church. Being universal in time as well as geography means that part of it is still here on earth–the Church Militant–while part of it has passed into the next life, where it consists of those who are still making progress–the Church Expectant–and those who have arrived–the Church Triumphant, not because it is revelling in some human triumph but because it is lost in wonder at the final triumph of God.

The Church asserts that the God who is Father of all and the Jesus Christ who accomplished these things and the Holy Spirit whom he sent to continue his work are all equally God yet there are not three Gods but one. It tries to reason this out in ways both inductive and deductive but always finds that at this point rationality becomes transcended in poetry and praise.

Being a human Society as well as a divine family, the Church needs organisation. Primary facet of this is a system of leadership. To establish the pattern of this, the Church of England looks back to the immediate friends of Jesus whom he charged to continue his work—the Apostles—and their early successors and discerns a threefold ministry of bishop, priest and deacon. It finds that while these people were to be leaders, their leadership was to be more of function than of dictatorial authority, for the character of the Christ whom they represent is servanthood not supremacy. His kingship is a ministry, not a mastery. The primary functions of these leaders are to be the constant expounding of God's statements, mostly made through Jesus Christ, and the servicing of the sacraments, the characteristic activities of the Society for which it looks to Jesus Christ as the source.

Being a human Society, this Church has to have its distinctive form of initiation, baptism (or *Christ*ening), and it has been guided to the conviction that since in this matter what God does is more important than what we do then it is right for infants to be given this privilege. This means that another ceremony, confirmation, is called for when these infants reach an age when they can answer for themselves. This, too, must have its right and proper form of administration.

There is no point in having a Society unless it has its own special activities. First among these is to be answerable to its origin, to be responsive to the God who brought it into being. Such response to God must always begin in praise and this praise is especially associated with commemorating the death and resurrection of Jesus on the first day of the week (when the resurrection happened) in the way that Jesus prescribed, the Eucharist, the taking, blessing, breaking and receiving of the bread which becomes his Body. Around this doing of the thing the Lord told us to do on the the Lord's day there grew up its attendant forms of corporate worship and these gain more substance from the private and personal forms of worship which each member offers privately in his own time.

This offering to God of worship further involves doing the things that God wants done and since he is above all a God who loves all he made, his followers must also love all. Vast works of charity done by the Society as a whole and tiny cups of water handed out personally by members of the Society to individuals in need must be the manward outreach of the worship which is Godward, and both the movement towards God and the movement towards man must be in one perfect harmony. The Church of England must at all times live in two dimensions, the vertical towards God and the horizontal towards all men. To hold what might appear contraries in accord is hard and there have been periods of history when one arm of the balance has apparently been submerged.

Such, obviously too scantily and inadequately, are the beliefs of the Church of England. But this statement immediately forces the question: are these the beliefs of the Church *of England* or are they the basic beliefs of Christendom (which in the twentieth century is not a geographical area but a worldwide attitude of mind)?

The answer is perhaps the most incisive that the Church of England ever makes on any point. This Church does not want to have any articles of faith which are peculiar to itself in the way, for example, that papal infallibility is peculiar to the Roman Catholic Church. There is no such thing as an *Anglican* theology. There are no special *Anglican* doctrines. For members of the Church of England there are only all the doctrines of the Christian Faith as they are found in the Bible, crystallised in the Creeds and expounded in the General Councils of the undivided Church.

To quote Archbishop Lord Fisher of Lambeth: 'There are no specifically Anglican doctrines. We hold as the faith only that which appears as such in the Scriptures and the Creeds. But there is a specifically Anglican temper of mind which our history has fashioned in us. Because of it we can hold out hands of understanding to Churches of every kind. Because of it, we are not afraid that association with others will compromise our own good name. It is, I think, part of our tradition that we are not self-conscious, or unduly even church-conscious, but conscious chiefly of the duty of the Church to be pursuing in Christ the unifying of truth, goodness and love, in witness to him and in a ministry to men. . . . We are, for the good of the universal Church, attempting the most difficult of all its internal problems – the due combination of order and freedom within the Church – and attempting it, not by running away from the tensions thereby created, but by meeting them in the spirit of Christ.'[1]

This book intends to be positive about the Church of England and not negative about other Churches. Yet there are points where we shall be forced to point contrasts and this is one of them.

One great mark of the Protestant Churches is that they can point to a historic moment when they found their identity. Thus Lutheranism looks back to 25 June 1630 when Emperor Charles V was presented with a statement of belief which both epitomised Christian doctrine as Luther saw it and also catalogued abuses which Luther wanted remedied. In other words, it was an excluding document. Anything not contained in its first half need not be required as part of the Faith and anything in its second half had to be abandoned. Similarly the great family of Churches which look to Calvin as founding father have a special moment and a source document to which they can always return for fresh inspiration and if need be, correction by its light. Until very recently a similar remark could be made about the Roman Catholic Church in that it had the Council of Trent and the first Vatican Council as the defining bodies which justified its detailed and precise catechism. The fact that not a few people have described Vatican II as an Anglicising occasion is significant here.

The Church of England has no great human name to which it returns for new inspiration. And it has no historic moment of beginning other than the beginning of Christianity itself. The Reformation, as I hope to show later, was no historic moment in

[1] *The Archbishop Speaks*, Evans, 1958, p. 80.

this sense. And it was by the Pope, not by any English authority, that Henry VIII was awarded his title of Defender of the Faith. Maybe the fact that the English Reformation never became a great historic moment was because Englishmen have little enthusiasm for taking anything to its logical conclusion. The doctrine of 'moderation in all things' has become an abiding strand of the English character and it undoubtedly had an influence when Englishmen gave their ancient Church a new look. The Reformation in England is a genuine *re*formation, not a new entity. The English Reformation was a matter of continuity, not contrast. Its exponents were men whose minds went instinctively to the Fathers of the early Church and not to the radicalism of the Protestant Continent or the reaction of the Counter-Reformation. They went to the patristic theology of the Greeks as well as the Romans and thus were saved from Western narrowness. And their approach to these pristine sources was not merely that of men who looked back to the undivided Church for their pattern but also that of sons in the Faith who claimed to be one with the undivided Church in continuity. The saintly Bishop Thomas Ken (died 1711) summed it up: 'I die in the Holy Catholic and Apostolic faith, professed by the whole Church before the division of East and West; more particularly I die in the Communion of the Church of England, as it stands distinguished from all papal and puritan innovations.' To that can be added the word of Sir Thomas Browne who gave us *Religio Medici*: 'I am of the Reformed newcast Religion, wherein I dislike nothing but the Name (i.e. Protestant. D.M.), of the same belief our Saviour taught, the Apostles disseminated, the Fathers authorised, and the Martyrs confirmed.'

The English Reformation is an episode in a sequence. Perhaps the key to the mind of the Church of England is to be found in that word 'sequence'. There is in the Anglican mind a deep conviction that the things of God are so infinitely bigger than we have yet realised. We have so very far to go before we shall know as we are known. In this sense, agnosticism in its purest meaning is a very legitimate Anglican attitude. There are so many things that we do not know. Yet this is no pessimistic agnosticism which folds its

7

hands and gives up trying to find out. For it is girded with the conviction that the God who loves must be a God who wants to be known, not through a glass darkly but face to face. And into the picture comes an element of patience and a readiness to accept half-truths and uncertainties as a temporary measure even while feeling bound to go probing beyond them. Thus all the 'don't-knows' of, say, a Bishop of Woolwich, are not the negative utterances of earthbound man but the exhilarating adventurings of a human soul. Anglicans are willing to admit that there are many things they do not know but they will never acquiesce in the suggestion that these things are finally unknowable or not worth knowing. The Church of England prefers pious opinion to alleged authoritative dogma. It esteems inquiry above infallibility.

The Church of England, indeed, takes this attitude to such a length that it seriously exposes itself to the critic and cartoonist. Its capacity for tolerating for the time being what appears to be error enables it to allow a Bishop Barnes to stay in Birmingham or a Dean Hewlett-Johnson to go on enjoying Canterbury, even when such men and their utterances manifestly cause scandal to many. It is easy for the outsider to construe such tolerance as an indifference to truth. It arises from exactly the opposite. Its source lies first in a conviction that truth is larger than we can conceive and we must always allow for it to have more facets than we can at present grasp. And its second source lies in a complete confidence that truth is big enough to look after itself and it must therefore be sought in all the cities and jungles rather than fenced up in some secure compound.

It is this which makes being a good Anglican a continued test of endurance. For Anglicanism does not say: make an act of faith in the Church as a final external authority and all will be well. It says: continue your pilgrimage, ever seeking. Even if you temporarily get on to the wrong road, go on searching.

Anglicanism is not a placid lake. It is a flowing river whose only goal is the total ocean. It is this which causes Anglicanism to be a constant matter of *becoming*. Protestanism is a great historical *event*, Anglicanism is the great historical process. Protestantism

comes back to the touchstone of 'back to the Reformers', Anglicanism wears pilgrim boots as it struggles on to find synthesis.

It is the validity of this search for a synthesis which makes
acceptable the paradoxes which so many condemn in the Church
of England. How, says the serious enquirer, can any organisation
be said to be an entity when it tries to include such various and
often directly conflicting opinions and practices? A familiar
enough gibe is that it contorts itself trying to hold together a
Catholic liturgy, a Calvinist set of Articles and an Erastian clergy.[1]
When Anglicans can be divided over their central beliefs–the
meaning of the presence of the Lord in the Eucharist, the necessity
or otherwise of having bishops–can they be united in anything?
The answer is that both these wings of thought and action are
legitimate expressions of men and they spring from the fact that
men are not all poured into one stereotyped mould. What Anglicanism seeks to do is to honour both wings and let both grow to
their fullest extent in the conviction that, like parallel lines, they
meet at the point of infinity. If an analogy is permissible, when
you walk up a valley the hills on either side seem to confront each
other with no hope that they will ever become one. But go up in a
helicopter and you see that both are part of an impressive mountain
system which has an integrity and meaning far beyond the sum of
the two hills.

Anglicanism walks in its valley–but it has no shadow of death
about it. It feels the tension of the two hills and it acknowledges
that it cannot properly look at both at the same time and appreciate
the strength and significance of each of them. But it does know that
they are ultimately not alien to each other. The Church of England
does not want to liquidate those who call themselves Protestants
and it could never consider losing its Catholic heritage. Instead it
accepts, with creative purpose not with resignation, the challenge
of letting–indeed, encouraging–both to grow together.

Dr Langmead Casserley has expressed it admirably: 'We may

---

[1] Erastianism is the doctrine that the State must dominate the Church in
ecclesiastical and all other matters. It derives from the Swiss, Thomas Erastus
(1524–83).

describe the movement of Anglican history as one from compromise to synthesis, from the middle way to the total way. It begins
by steering cautiously between two extremes but we can already
see, in the light of more than four centuries of history, that it can
only end by comprehending the two extremes, by including two
points of view which, through a series of lamentable historical
accidents, have come to interpret themselves as antithetical, in one
rich, coherent synthesis which will enable us to recover the
wholeness of the Catholic Faith.'[1]

It is this which makes the Church of England guardian of a
dialectic faith in which logical disputation can happen without
ill-mannered dissension. It is the sort of debate which gives each
side the right to maintain the full truth as it sees it. There have been
times in history when enthusiasm has degenerated into fanaticism
and each side of the debate has resorted to violence, to appeal to
the law, or even to the arbitration of the Judicial Committee of the
Privy Council. The partisan spirit has indeed had its field days and
blood sports they were. Especially in the latter half of the nineteenth century when platform and pulpit became more accustomed
to polemics than to peaceful preaching. The object of each group
then was, quite simply, to excommunicate the other and the means
they adopted became a scandal not only to the faithful but to any
sane person. But those days have gone, not because either side has
surrendered its truth, indeed, those truths may be even more
strongly held today, but because each group has realised that the
total Gospel is richer than it thought and has many elements. This
fact was realised even in the New Testament itself. Two adjoining
Epistles, for example, Hebrews and James, give very different
pictures of the Christian Faith if taken in isolation from each
other. And there seems little in common between the stern logic of
the Epistle to the Romans and the mystic love of the Johannine
epistles or between the reportage of Acts and the visionary soaring
of The Revelation.

The party spirit has very long roots and very far-reaching consequences. It can even be argued that the party spirit has been one

---

[1] *Christian Community*, p. 111.

of the strengths of Anglicanism. Each side has kept the other on its toes. Each has had continually to go back to its foundations and re-examine them. There has been no *Roma locuta, causa finita* to lead to complacent acceptance. Always men of goodwill will find themselves impelled to find the synthesis and in doing so they will be seeking to reconcile the wings not of Anglicanism *per se* but of the whole of Christendom.

There is also another angle on this, well expressed by Bishop J. W. C. Wand: 'In any case, it is difficult to see why as schools of thought there should be any internecine conflict between the two. The psychological, biblical approach of the evangelical with its emphasis on faith, conversion and atonement need not exclude the ontological, sacramental approach of the catholic with its emphasis on grace, authority and the incarnation. St. Paul certainly held both the psychological and the biological elements together without any sense of incongruity.'[1]

Over all, the continuing discussion has been civilised and searching and it is certainly so today. But there has been enough disagreement and acknowledgement of disagreement to prove that the Anglican ideal, whatever its critics may say, is not compromise but comprehension. It is not passive acceptance for the sake of peace but dynamic activity for the sake of perfection. To accept the battle of opposites is not a death-wish but a life-force. Perhaps it has best been summed up in the Report of the Committee on Unity in the Lambeth Conference of 1948:[2] 'The co-existence of these divergent views within the Anglican Communion sets up certain tensions; but these are tensions within a wide range of agreement in faith and practice. We recognise the inconvenience caused by these tensions, but we acknowledge them to be part of the will of God for us, since we believe that it is only through a comprehensiveness which makes it possible to hold together in the Anglican Communion understandings of truth which are held in separation in other Churches, that the Anglican Communion is able to reach out in different directions and so to fulfil its special

---

[1] *Anglicanism in History and Today,* Weidenfeld & Nicolson, 1961.
[2] pp, 50–51.

vocation as one of God's instruments for the restoration of the visible unity of his whole Church. If at the present time one view were to prevail to the exclusion of all others, we should be delivered from our tensions, but only at the price of missing our opportunity and our vocation.'

All this has given English religious thinking a character of its own. The Germans have built up massive systems of theology painstakingly worked out with intellectual precision and infinite labour. The English have sought to be more practical and to remove their theology from the university to the market place. It can be said that English theologians are more amateur, in the sense that fewer of them devote their whole time to theology. The present Archbishop of Canterbury, Dr Ramsey, is an example of such. Few would deny him a place among the first flight of theologians. But anyone who bears the burden of Lambeth can hardly have much time to give to the study and the research library. The Anglican scholar's intellectual efforts have usually been somewhere near to pastoral concerns and he has therefore been quick to see the practical relevance and to pursue it. Somehow his theology has not suffered—else how did *Clerus Anglicanus stupor mundi* become so widespread a tag? Yet he has never let his theology become the aery void which was the ultimate fate of scholasticism.

The combination of the acceptance of opposites with this relaxed approach to theology has led to an Anglican patience with the other man's opinion. Lest this may be thought something which has arisen as the fruit of some twentieth-century indifferentism, we call seventeenth-century Archbishop Laud as witness. Dr Norman Sykes has said, 'If Laud stood for a fixed liturgy and uniformity of rites and ceremonies, he championed also a free pulpit; whilst his opponents stood for a free liturgy and a rigid theological system.'[1] Voltaire was being very Anglican when he said, 'I disapprove of what you say, but I will defend to the death your right to say it.'

But the picture of Anglican belief which is growing on these pages could be construed as a pathless jungle where each may hack away in whatever direction his fancy takes him. That would be

[1] *The English Religious Tradition*, S.C.M. Press, p. 38.

misleading. For Anglicans do have some guidelines. Most obvious, but probably least useful, of these is the document known as *The Thirty-nine Articles*, subject of argument and casual dismissal for so long. Back in the sixteenth century the Church of England, more than usually in need to establish its identity, saw many doctrinal statements produced, some of them very positive about what to believe, some of them merely negative in asserting what was wrong with other people's beliefs. *The Thirty-nine Articles* in their present form date from 1571, the year in which Parliament made it mandatory that all candidates for ordination should publicly and formally subscribe to them, such subscription having to be repeated each time a man was presented to a new benefice. Parliament's object was to produce a unified kingdom and to that end the Articles were contrived to relieve Puritan scruples. Such concessions made little appeal to Catholic minds but they also failed to satisfy people like the stricter Calvinists who wanted more precise definition on such matters as predestination and total depravity.

'The Articles were evidently not meant as, nor were they ever claimed to be, a complete systematic statement of Christian truth; they had the more limited aim of determining questions – some of them, certainly, very important questions – which disturbed the peace of the Church in the mid-sixteenth century.'[1] The Articles, in other words, were a response to a given historical situation and both their cogency and their relevance diminished as that situation got further and further into the past. The Articles cannot be taken as reflecting the mind of the Church of England today and the question of the clergy subscribing to them has long been abandoned in favour of their 'assenting' instead. The difference between subscribe and assent is roughly that the former means the detailed acceptance of the Articles as currently valid statements while to assent is to approve the Articles in principle in their historic setting while at the same time insisting that their interpretation be made in the light of other documents, notably the Bible, the Creeds,

---

[1] *Subscription and Assent to the 39 Articles*, Report of the Archbishops' Commission, S.P.C.K. 1968, p. 10.

the Book of Common Prayer and the Ordinal. The latest in a series of Commissions on this subject published its Report (mentioned above) in 1968 and, in a somewhat guarded Anglican way, gave its approval to the idea of assent.

But Commissions may meet and reach conclusions. The simple fact is that, apart from fleeting glances during a boring sermon, Anglicans rarely look at *The Thirty-nine Articles*. Even if they had the capacity to form the basis of Anglican belief they would remain esoteric. And if they were not, if, that is, they were widely accepted, then they would be alien to Anglicanism for their effect is to exclude others. The Articles are interesting but only as museum pieces reflecting some of the tensions of the Church four hundred years ago. Where, then, do Anglicans look for their beliefs?

Supremely the answer is: in the Bible which is the charter document and the final arbiter. But even here Anglicanism has to have a qualifying clause.

The Bible is a book which the simplest can read and derive meaning from and it is also a book which baffles the most scholarly. In other, words, it is a book too big for an individual to assimilate on his own. Attempts to do so have led to prostituting it into a form of idolatry as blasphemous as any other substitition for God. It has been treated as a magic book—stick a pin into its pages and get the infallible guidance you need. It has been made a substitute for the astrologer. It has been distorted by selectivity. It has been made an ogre by suggesting that its every word is totally inerrant, even when its original language is translated by fallible men.

The main stream of Christendom has always recognised these dangers. And it has found in the source of the Bible the safeguards against them. Quite simply, the Bible, and more especially the New Testament, was written by churchmen to churchmen and for churchmen. And it was the Church which was responsible for the decision about which books should be included in the Bible and which should be left out. It is therefore implicit that the Bible should be read by Churchmen and that the Church should have a hand in its interpretation. To treat it as a sole authority is to wrench it from its context.

The Church of England has no doubt about the authority, supreme in its own area, of the Bible. 'Holy Scripture containeth all things necessary to salvation: so that whatsoever is not read therein, nor may be proved thereby, is not to be required of any man that it should be believed as an article of the Faith, or to be thought requisite or necessary to salvation.' (In this quotation, Bible means the Old and New Testaments. The Church, according to Anglicans, reads the Apocrypha 'for example of life and instruction of manners; but it doth not apply it to establish any doctrine'.)

It was this open, available, commended Bible which was the greatest gift of the English Reformation and it has probably been the greatest moulding agent on the life and literature of England ever since.

Anglicans have always recognised the unique authority of the Bible. But at the same time they have also recognised that it is capable of variety of interpretation. And they have remembered that even in the New Testament the difficulty of the Bible on its own was recognised. No Scripture, said the second epistle of St Peter, is 'of private interpretation'. 'How can I understand unless some man guide me?' asked the Ethiopian Eunuch in the Acts. There is only one safeguard against personal whim and partisan selection in the use of the Bible and that is the Church itself. A controversy about the Scripture and its interpretation can hardly be decided within the Scripture itself. It cannot be both judge and defendant. Therefore the Bible must be subjected to the principles of the faith, to the corporate memory which is tradition and to reason. And what better communal representation of these is there than the Church?

So the simple Anglican formula developed: the Church to teach and the Bible to prove. It is worth noting that this formula is roughly the one which reproduces the normal pattern of human life. Religion is first taught us by our parents–as representatives of the Church–and subsequently we go to the authorities to check what they said.

Perhaps the final resolution of the ancient argument about

which is superior, Bible or Church, was produced by the 1958 Lambeth Conference: 'Neither Bible nor Church is understood apart from the other. . . . The Church is the witness and keeper of Holy Writ, charged to interpret it and expound it by the aid of the Spirit of truth which is in the Church. But, on the other hand, the Church is not "over" the Holy Scriptures but "under" them in the sense that the process of canonisation (the selection of the Books of the Bible) was not one whereby the Church conferred authority on the books but one whereby the Church acknowledged them to possess authority. And why? The books were recognised as giving the witness of the Apostles to the life, teaching, death and Resurrection of the Lord and the interpretation by the Apostles of these events. To that apostolic authority the Church must ever bow.'[1]

What Anglicans say is that there is no question of weighing the Bible and the Church against each other and assessing grades of importance and authority. For both Bible and Church are extrapolations of Christ who is the sole and supreme Authority. Both Church and Bible derive their meaning from his profundity.

Anglicans, then, will seek to establish their beliefs by reading the Bible and listening to the Church. But they also have another uniquely important document. It is the Book of Common Prayer. No Church, and possibly no human organisation in history, has had a single more formative handbook (other than the Bible) than this treasured companion of millions of devout souls. Another chapter is going to be concerned in more detail about this Prayer Book but one point must be made here. The point is more than relevant. It is the heart of our search for Anglican beliefs.

The practical nature of Anglican theology has created a condition of mind which is convinced that considerations about God (which is all that theology is) must never be an academic matter but must infuse the whole being of man and be infused by it. It has therefore been taken out of the colleges and the cloisters and given living expression. Thus the beliefs of Anglicans are not contained in some

[1] *Report*, pp. 2.3 and 2.4.

dry formulary which commends itself only to the intellect but instead they have been enshrined in the continuing activity of prayer. Anglicans do not define God. Instead they address him and in doing so they dwell on his characteristics. They do not issue official treatises on what Christian marriage is about. Instead they enshrine all their thoughts on the subject in the prayers and vows which make up the Marriage Service. The Anglican who wants to know what his Church thinks about baptism or whatever turns first to his Prayer Book to see how these things happen and what is the implication of the actions as well as the words involved. Anglicanism has realised, perhaps to a unique degree, that all orthodoxy issues in doxology. Anglicans feel they get further into the mystery of the Blessed Trinity by saying 'Glory be to the Father and to the Son and to the Holy Ghost, as it was in the beginning, is now and ever shall be' than they would by many hours of cogitation about the nature of this supreme doctrine. In enshrining its doctrines in living prayer rather than in arid documents the Church of England follows very closely the mood of the Creeds commonly accepted by all Churches. For they do not say 'There is one God. . . .' Rather they ask the human being to say 'I believe in one God. . . .' This is a concrete statement but even more it is a personal commitment. The Creed is not concerned with some remote intellectual brainchild Deity but with the approach to a personal God.

Faith, in other words, becomes part of life. It is not just an intellectual process but transcends that to become part of the fibre of a man's being. You can be casual about any detailed enunciation and precise articulation of your beliefs when they have become part of your general climate of thought. Anglicanism has its own atmosphere, its own attitude, rather than a faith of its own.

This transformation of thought into activity leads on to what has been regarded by many as the supreme mark of the Anglican. A Norwegian Lutheran, Dr Einar Molland, has expressed it superbly: 'If selection were to be made of a particular doctrine as specially characteristic of the Anglican Communion as a whole, it would certainly be the theology of the Incarnation. While other

Churches emphasise the Resurrection of Christ or the Atonement, the Anglican Communion regards the Incarnation, the doctrine of the Son of God made man for us men and for our salvation, as the central theme of Christian theology. If the Orthodox Church is the 'Church of Easter', or the Lutheran Church the 'Church of Good Friday', the Anglican Church may be described as the 'Church of Christmas'.[1]

The Incarnation is about God leaving his inaccessible places and coming down to earth. Jesus Christ did not spend time defining himself. He went about praising God and doing good. Anglicanism has sought after this down-to-earth quality. It has noted that, as St John has it, 'the Word became flesh and dwelt among us' and has tried to enflesh its own words. When that Word became flesh the Son of God accepted limitations. Anglicanism has always been aware that it lacks omnicompetence. When the Son of God became man he accepted the pressure and limitations of external circumstances. The Anglican Church has certainly followed in that respect – which is perhaps why the same Dr Molland can describe it as 'the most elastic Church in Christendom'.

The central doctrine of the Incarnation is that Jesus Christ was both Perfect God and perfect man. Holding these two apparently irreconcilable statements in balance has been the hardest task of all for Christians. Where does the God part end and the man part begin and vice versa? That is the sort of question which agonises. Alongside that and directly related to it is the question: where in life in general does the secular end and the sacred begin? Anglicans have never really understood that question nor have they seen it as having real significance. They have never really distinguished between the sacred and the profane for they are convinced that all life is of God and that he does not divide it up into categories. This has led to a mood which the critics have defined as worldliness and has provided much inspiration for cartoonists in *Punch* and other social observers. It is important enough to deserve our attention.

The most quoted of all key texts in the Gospels is 'God so loved the world that he gave his only-begotten Son.' So many people

[1] *Christendom*, Mowbrays, 1959. p. 148.

fail to note that it is the *world*, not any Church nor any in-group, which is the object of God's love. Perhaps then we can legitimately describe God as being 'worldly'. What Anglicans have insisted on is that not one jot of all creation can be yielded to any other power than God's. Every sparrow is his and the devil has no right whatsoever even to the worst tunes, let alone the best. Jesus went to Temple and synagogue. But he also graced the parties of publicans and sinners. He went *everywhere*–doing good. The matter was perhaps best summed up by William Temple when he said that Christianity is the most material of all religions. What else could it be when it begins with the proposition that God accepted a human, material body? Christianity is ineluctably a sacramental religion and that inevitably means involvement in the world. The Bread which we break was made in a worldly oven.

Yet this very worldliness can have its weaknesses, especially to a mind which seeks in religion an escapism from the harshness of life. The Amish folk in the U.S.A. may confine themselves to their iron-less lumbering covered waggons with their long-bearded men looking neither to left or right as they go. For them, primitive and isolated living is a creed encapsulated in the world's most sophisticated civilisation. They keep themselves to themselves and seek their own salvation while the rest of the world goes by. Anglicans cannot. There are some who seek the security of such strait-jacketed finality. Because Anglicans do not provide this, they inevitably lose in terms of definition. You know what an Amish is about. You have to keep on guessing about an Anglican. You know how an Amish will react to a situation. An Anglican's response usually remains an unknown quantity. You can identify an Amish by his dress. An Anglican gets lost in the crowd.

Such things may make an Anglican appear colourless and characterless. They are certainly limiting. But there is also a very positive side. When the Word became flesh, he became total man. And, impressively, he made his appeal to total man. He did not patronise men by giving them lucid and final answers to their questions. He gave them guidelines and let them attain maturity by coming to the fulness of truth in their own way. Perhaps the

C   19

most astonishing feature of the Gospels is the way in which Jesus waited until men were ready before he led them on to a new truth. He did not brush aside as trivial their doubts, he did not over-ride their consciences as they had come to be formed, nor did he dismiss all their previous life as being irrelevant. Thomas was given special attention when he had his problems about belief, the men who took a woman in adultery were not told that their consciences should be aware that there might be worse sins, Matthew was not asked to forget all his financial expertise when he was called to follow. Jesus came not to destroy but to fulfil.

Underlying all that last paragraph there are three key words. Reason, conscience, experience. These have been the three key words which have informed all Anglican thinking. But they have a much more fundamental force than that. They are the three key elements which any man brings into operation when he takes a responsible decision.

Although he does not always live up to his high calling, man is a rational animal. He is a creature with a mind, with the faculty for directing a living organism towards a particular goal. This involves looking at the other available goals and making a selection. The mind is an enduring part of man. Socrates' body has long since disintegrated but his mind continues its influence. Anglicanism takes full account of this reasoning faculty. It asks that reason shall be brought to bear on religion. It accepts Plato's dictum that 'the unexamined life is unliveable for a human being' and argues that since that is true for man's lower nature it is *a fortiori* cogent for his higher life. This does not imply that the reason is powerful enough to take us right into the heart of the nature of God. It still leaves room for the exercise of faith. But Anglicanism has always accepted what the Scriptures insist upon, that faith is always the antonym of sight, not of reason. Anglicanism, therefore, has always been able to say to the scientist and to the researcher, Bless you, go on with your investigations. The nearer you get to truth the nearer you get to God.

The magnificent scientific record of the English people owes no small debt to the nature of the Church of England.

But reason is not man's only faculty. Alongside it always must go his conscience. Deep down in the nature of man is a sense of obligation to some law higher than his own desires. Generation by generation, judgements about what is right and what is wrong may vary but the conviction that there is an ultimate and enduring difference between right and wrong remains. Conscience is the point at which man is in touch with whatever is final in the universe. The Church of England has always insisted that the conscience of an individual remains inviolable–though not ineducable to higher stages. It has a final authority even though it may lack finality. This conviction has inevitably led to an apparent chaos of Anglican activity for it means that Anglicanism has never been able to develop an impressive corpus of moral case law and impose it on all who seek membership. Casuistry, the laying down of ethical rules to special cases and the classification of particular offences and their exceptions, is a perfectly legitimate study. But in the English language the word has acquired pejorative meanings since it implies that someone else is going to take over a man's conscience and exercise his moral obligations for him and Anglicans have taught the English mind to resent that. The Anglican parson is one who knows that human nature is so complex that it cannot be shoe-horned into hidebound categories. His task in advising on a moral situation therefore is to state the relevant principles and then insist that the individuals concerned act like adults and take their own decisions. In this, as in so much else, this Church insists on treating people as if they were mature. Frequently they are recognisably not, but if their swaddling bands are kept tight they never will be.

Reason and conscience are supremely important. Yet they limp without the presence of the third factor, experience. It is important to get the full meaning of this word in this context. It includes all the things a man has learned in the course of his life but it also goes much further and brings in the whole revelation of God as transmitted to a man especially through the Bible and the Church. In other words, it treats a man's experience as being the sum total of his memory added to the corporate memory of the Christian

Society. It recognises that a man will frequently find himself in a situation where his own experience gives little guidance. It is then his duty to give even more careful consideration to the vast treasuries of the experience of others which is available to him.

Reason, conscience, experience. It is obvious that there are many times when one or more of these seem to be in direct conflict. Experience, for example, may have proved that to follow one's conscience is painful. Yet the whole art of living for any man consists in bringing the three into harmony and letting each of the three attain its fullest potential. To do so may be an agonising process. Anglicanism recognises that and it also acknowledges that, in insisting that each individual seeks this end it is laying itself open to apparent inconsistencies and chaos. It accepts the fact because it knows that life is not a precooked ready-to-serve recipe, but a challenge to everything a man has the power to become. And it knows that at the heart of its faith, as at the heart of life, there is paradox. For Christians this paradox is the seemingly supremely absurd statement that the death of a felon on a cross nearly two thousand years ago was the final act of God Almighty reconciling all things to himself. If one can swallow that camel then every Anglican inconsistency looks like a very small gnat.

2

Praying

'Let me come into the church of God to meet the Spirit of God: not to give religion an hour, but to live in the eternal.'
Eric Milner-White *My God my Glory*

As the last chapter indicated, there is no easy formula for expressing Anglican ways of thinking. To describe Anglican spirituality presents even greater problems. This is not surprising. For processes of thought, however elevated, are only *about* God. Spirituality is the exercise of the soul approaching God. Access to the Infinite must be along many paths and each of them has its own intimations of infinity. Making a map is difficult.

Again, a process of thought, even when corporately accepted as in a creed, remains an individual thing. Spirituality, on the other hand, has both its private and its public moments of expression. Each is essential to the other, each intertwines with the other. To break them into categories and write about them coherently is not easy.

Spirituality must be the hardest of all human activities to formulate. It is open equally to the simplest rustic and to the most sage academic. Indeed, in some mysterious manner it goes even further, for the Bible tells us that 'the heavens declare the glory of God and the firmament showeth his handiwork'. All created things, animate and inanimate, have their place in the act of praise which is the highest reach of spirituality.

Again, spirituality has no single face. It can be drawn in the tearful lines of penitence or in the humility of intercession, it can soar into the heights of thanksgiving or into the ecstasy of the worship of God for his own sake without thought of all his gifts. In the underside of spirituality you can detect the threads of every human condition and every human emotion.

23

But perhaps the supreme thing about spirituality in that it is totally uninhibited by circumstances. The prisoner in a concentration camp or an invalid on the point of death has little chance of doing works of mercy. He is unlikely to have books on which to sharpen his theological knowledge. But the confinement of the body does nothing to hinder the journeying of the soul into spirituality. It is a land of open doors and there are neither passports nor visas required. It is a land which is always there and also is there for always. One can conceive the time when all human thought will have ceased. But spirituality, for the Christian, partakes of the eternity of God, the only source of eternity. That thought leads us to its heart. Spirituality, especially as expressed in worship, is not a process we begin nor can it be something we have invented. It is a ceaseless activity into which we enter, whether as individuals or as a group. This is true for all Christians. But have we anything especially Anglican to say on the subject?

Whether for moments of private devotion or for great corporate acts, whether for grief at a death or for joy at a marriage, whether in humble village church or in magnificent cathedral, it is to one source that the Anglican instinctively turns: The Book of Common Prayer. Along with the Bible, of which it is the synopsis, this Book has been pre-eminently the moulding factor of the English language and its phrases come readily even when no book is available— the *Oxford Dictionary of Quotations* rates several hundred of them worthy of inclusion. This is the Book in which Anglicans aimed to enshrine everything they fought to recover at the Reformation. Yet it is no invention of the Reformation.

Without in any way diminishing the importance of private devotion, the great characteristic of any Christian community is corporate prayer culminating in observing the Lord's command to break bread together in remembrance of him. In parenthesis, there is one problem of nomenclature we must clear immediately. This heart of Christian worship has developed many names 'The Lord's Supper', 'The Breaking of the Bread', 'The Mass', 'The Holy Mysteries', 'The Eucharist', 'The Holy Communion' and so on. All of them mean the same thing yet the moulding of history has given all of them overtones. To some degree each of them has been associated with some part of the Church and has accordingly acquired some particular theological emphasis. In this chapter therefore we shall largely avoid using any one of them, if only because all are quite legitimately used in the Church of England.

Christians have always gathered together for worship – the Greek word *'ecclesia'* means an assembly of people called out of the general public. *The Acts of the Apostles* is full of such phrases as 'being assembled together', 'all continued with one accord in prayer and supplication', 'continued steadfastly in the apostles' doctrine and fellowship, and in breaking of bread, and in prayers'. The Lord's promise that 'Where two or three are gathered together in my name, there am I in the midst of them' has been taken seriously. Christianity, which is nothing if it is not a social religion, finds its highest social expression in corporate worship. It therefore follows the example of its Lord whose private devotions found focal points in visits to synagogue and temple. Corporate worship is a Christian must.

But how? There are two answers. Corporate worship can either be spontaneous or it can follow a formal pattern. At first sight the spontaneous would seem to have much to commend it. It appears less vulnerable to insincerity and boredom. It is more able to meet the needs of the moment. Yet the great majority of Christians have chosen formality and set formulae. They have remembered first of all that when Jesus' advice was sought he gave a very clear set of words. Say 'Our Father who art . . .' he said. He gave those words not as a catalogue from which items could be selected but to be used as a complete whole. Maybe there would be times when we would be more concerned about being delivered from evil than about hallowing God's name. But prayer was to depend on eternal verities, not on passing moods.

The pattern of Christian worship was set in the Lord's prayer. Following its principles Christians have from the earliest days used set forms of prayer. How else could the excellence of God be approached except by the best and most carefully chosen words? True, God would not let the efficacy of prayer depend on the literary qualities of its phrasing. But could a worshipper offer him anything less than the best? Again, to use carefully prepared forms allows one to range over all previous spiritual manuals, an exercise which not only offers a treasury of literary form but also gives access to a breadth of spiritual experience such as no individual achieves. It is to accept the promise that the Spirit will lead us into all truth and that, generation by generation, more and more will be revealed. To prepare one's prayers by a consideration of the fruits of the spiritual achievements of others is not only to gain the pragmatic truth of a form which has proved valuable but also the inner truth which that form has embodied.

To use written prayers is in itself an act of worship since it acknowledges that God is a God of order. It reaches its highest form when we find that the next thing in the book is not merely what we *have* to say but is really what we *want* to say because it is the one and only right thing to say at that moment. It is then that spontaneity and formality marry and a new experience is born. No longer does devotion depend on whim or feeling, no longer is it strait-jacketed by a single fumbling tongue. Instead it enshrines all humanity and finds a freedom of words loved into sanctity by generations.

There is another point. Corporate worship, if it is to be meaningful, must be the prayers of the whole congregation even though they be spoken through the lips of one person. Public worship does not consist in listening to someone pray and wondering what he is going to say next. It means knowing the words in anticipation and sharing in them as each is spoken. The minister whose spontaneous words impress a congregation too easily becomes an end in himself and a barrier between God and the worshipper. Even the monotonous drone of a man who has lost interest in the words can prove no worse a leader of worship than the verbal fireworks of an orator which rivet attention to themselves. Indeed, in much of its worship the Church deliberately depersonalises the minister by requiring him to intone words rather than speak them with his own personal emphases and inflexions. Thus does he stop being an individual and become the impartial voice of the whole.

But behind and beyond all this there lies a still more important theological truth. Our prayers are not something we do in isolation. It is the Spirit who prays in us. The Spirit is at his constant work of prayer and our prayers must be our way of letting him pray in us and speak through our lips. No man can call Jesus Lord, but by the Spirit. Prayer is the mysterious encounter between God and ourselves and the initiative is taken by God who comes to meet us when we open ourselves to let him in. When we use the words of others in a printed book we are trying to experience the best of the distilled essence of the whole Christian community of the experience of the Spirit praying within it over the centuries.

Worship, if it is to be worship, can never be self-centred, whether the self be a minister or a congregation. Its nature is to be objective. And objectivity is best secured by going outside oneself and using forms which have proved acceptable through use and custom. Thus from the earliest years there grew up formularies.

Broadly speaking these formularies for public worship fell into two groups. There were those which were related to the Lord's command to break bread in remembrance of him. All of them had a common allegiance to the four great verbs of the Lord's action— he took bread, blessed it, broke it and gave it. In other respects they showed great diversity, not a little derived from local national characteristics. Thus in the early Christian centuries one finds such rites as the Mozarabic, belonging to the Spanish peninsula and used there until the eleventh century, and the Ambrosian, associated with Milan. These together with the Celtic forms were clearly distinguishable from the Roman rite and are known generically as the Gallican rite. A primary difference is that the Gallican family types are more flowery in their language than the more austere Roman form. Maybe this difference arises from the possibility that the Gallican rite derived from the more expressive eastern Mediterranean. The idea that there has always been one standard Roman rite from which others have deviated is illusory. But the Roman rite has always powerfully sought to establish itself as the norm. Thus when Augustine arrived in England in 597 he found remains of the Celtic rite. By 603 he had summoned all

Christians in England to accept the Roman rite and half a century later at the Synod of Whitby in 664 the Roman rite won the day. Even so, Wales and Ireland persisted with their ancient forms which long predated Augustine.

To say that the Roman rite ever acquired a monopoly in England is misleading. As late as medieval times the great cathedrals of Hereford, York, Lincoln, Bangor and Salisbury had their own significant variations.

We have been speaking thus far of the central service of the Christian faith, the response to the Lord's command to receive his Body in remembrance. It is the heart point. Yet it must not be allowed to overshadow the other parts of the public worship gathered under the title of the Divine Office–the word 'office' emphasising that it is an obligation accepted by the clergy. These services derive from a proper reverence for the Holy Mysteries which suggested they should be surrounded by preparatory and subsequently thanksgiving prayer. This led the Church to remember that the people of the Old Testament observed fixed hours of prayer. 'Seven times a day will I praise thee', said the Psalmist. Thus there grew up the 'offices' to mark the hours of the day, Mattins, Lauds, Prime, Terce, Sext, None, Vespers and Compline. Their basic content, prayers, psalms and readings, followed the ancient synagogue pattern.

It was the great St Benedict in Monte Cassino in the first half of the sixth century who gave them their final pattern. For him it was the *opus Dei*. As such it deserved man's best attention and elaboration until, as Cranmer was to write, 'The number and hardness of the rules and the manifold changings of the service was the cause that to turn the book only was so hard and intricate a matter, that many times there was more business to find out what should be read than to read it when it was found out.'

All of which meant that for the man in the pew public worship had become an intricate and highly professional matter. And he could hardly be blamed if he resorted to his own private devotions, many of them superstitions, especially since there were few sermons to teach him anything else. Nevertheless, as Bishop Moorman has said, 'In his own inner life the average Englishman of the later Middle Ages was undoubtedly religious . . . the English as a whole were a religious nation and impressed foreign visitors as such.'[1] The sale of books of private devotion supports that. Between 1478 and 1534 no fewer than 116 editions of the *Sarum Primer* were printed in Latin and in the next thirteen years there were 28 editions printed in English.

Printed. The word is significant. For this new (to Europe) invention was a powerful force to explode men's minds into a new era. Reformation was in the air. Whether or not there would have been a clearing of the jungle of public worship without the other incentives to change is a fascinating question but it is purely academic. Christian worship is not a series of mechanical formulae but a relationship with the living God. It therefore cannot remain static. It grows. All the conditions for growth were present.

In England, as another chapter notes more closely, the Reformation had major political overtones. Yet, significantly, the acme of its expression was in a Prayer Book. This is more natural than at first sight appears. For every human society seems to believe that political orthodoxy is best gained and sustained through religious conformity – Roman Emperor worship was a good example and so is Soviet Russia. It was this conviction which was to cause England's Prayer Book to be captured by the State and remain chained to its Parliament. But this mood was no peculiarity of an island people. In the same generation as we were having our first Book of Common Prayer, Olaus Petri was preparing one in Sweden, one was being published in Finland and the redoutable Luther issued his ordinances for reformed worship. Even the Roman Church was thinking of revision of forms of worship. Cardinal Quignon had drawn up a Breviary which gained the approval of the Council of Trent in 1545.

The important feature about the English Reformation is that it deliberately and successfully set out to be a break not with the Catholic Faith but with the Pope. By the time of Henry VIII's death, the first authorised translation of the English Bible was, by

---

[1] *A History of the Church in England*, A. & C. Black, 1953, p. 156.

royal command, to be found in all churches and it was to be read 'openly' every Sunday but there was still no Book of Common Prayer. That was to wait until 1549 and the strangely ambivalent genius of Cranmer. Cranmer, made Archbishop of Canterbury by Henry in 1533, is the man about whom everyone takes sides, for or against, but always violently. Fortunately, for the moment anyway, we are not called to assess him here. All we need to know is that he was probably the finest liturgical scholar of his day, with a wide knowledge of the public prayer of the eastern as well as the western church and an ability to read fluently Latin, Greek, Hebrew, French, German and Italian. Moreover, his love for language was sensitised by an ear for its music. This man, who must have grown impatient at constantly being dragged into the public arena, produced, almost in his spare time, one of the greatest of all companions to worship. To it he brought all the treasury of Christian devotion which he distilled. The continuity of the English Church finds a continuity of prayer and praise through Cranmer's gifts. And the first Prayer Book was published at three shillings and eight pence the piece.

The Book of Common Prayer is a profound aesthetic experience. Yet Cranmer was not one to leave it in the realm of emotion. The Prayer Book had to speak to the minds of men also. So almost every service was given its Exhortation and the whole thing is permeated with the Bible. And as a result G. M. Trevelyan can say, 'When Elizabeth came to the throne the Bible and the Prayer Book formed the intellectual and spiritual foundation of the new order.' There is, indeed, almost a false dichotomy about mentioning Bible and Prayer Book as separate entities for if the Prayer Book were deprived of the Bible it would have little left. The Holy Communion service, for example, is emaciated without its regular Epistles and Gospels while Mattins and Evensong look to the Bible not only for the Lessons and the Psalms (recited completely every month) but also for most of the great Canticles which have always been their highlights—and which have inspired composers to such musical achievements. Thus there are six sizeable portions of scripture set every day in the course of ordinary routine. 'The

Eucharist is illuminated by the Scriptures; and the power of the Scriptures is enhanced by their use in the Eucharist', said a Lambeth Conference, and again 'The Word in the Scriptures is the more vivid on account of the nearness of Jesus who is the Word in sacramental presence and gift.' An essential part of the Prayer Book is the Lectionary which takes its user through the Old Testament once a year and through the New Testament twice. The classical statement of Anglican thinking, as we have already noted, is 'The Church to teach, the Bible to prove'. The statement about its public worship could well be; 'The Church to pray, the Bible to provide the content of prayer.' The Bible is God speaking to his people. The Prayer Book is some of his people trying to reply.

The Book of Common Prayer was published in 1549. More than that, the Act of Uniformity which became law on 21 January that year imposed its exclusive use from the following Whit Sunday 'in the celebrations of the Lord's Supper, commonly called the Mass' and in all public services. The parson who refused to comply was subject to forfeiture of a year's income and six months' imprisonment for a first offence, with deprivation and a year's imprisonment for a second offence and with imprisonment for life if he had still failed to learn his lesson. There were also penalties for 'depraving' or speaking against the Prayer Book. And all services were to be in English—except at the universities where they could use other languages 'for the sake of learning'.

The 1549 Prayer Book was indeed given a powerful start in life. But perhaps it did not need it. Like all its successors, it offered a universal guide to spirituality and it has gone round the world through the Churches of the Anglican Communion. Distilling the spiritual treasuries of the ages its primary provision is the Lord's own service in response to his command to break the bread and the ancillary 'offices'. Very significantly Cranmer took the great eight services of the monastic round and distilled them into two, Mattins and Evensong. He thus released them from the confines of the clergy and let them run loose in the minds and souls of princes and peasants. They still remained the obligation of the clergy but they now became the treasury of the laity also. To the regular daily round, Cranmer added those things needed on occasion – his incomparable Litany and the services which mark life's great moments like baptism, marriage and death. Thus can a man read the promise made in his name when he was baptised or husband and wife can renew their marriage vows as each anniversary occurs. Thus, too, can any individual, ordained or lay, find the common fare of spiritual sustenance. Thus, in fact, are all the mysteries of religion brought out of the sanctuary and on to the hearth so that every Englishman has his own access into holiness. Perhaps one reason why the English are bad at going to church is because the Church has so successfully gone to them. An illustration of the way the Prayer Book became the property of the common man is that by 1550 John Merbecke had hunted the hedges and found folktunes for musical settings to it. Thus did a sixteenth-century Folk Mass become the image of 'church music' in our day.

It is tempting to linger over Cranmer's Prayer Book. But history did not. It lasted four years only.

'The First Prayer Book', writes Percy Dearmer, 'was indeed too fair-minded for the violent and bitter spirit of the age. Our Book of Common Prayer has been like a ship launched on a troublous sea. The ship was shattered before the end of this reign, sunk in that of Mary, refitted when Elizabeth began to reign, wrecked in the storms of the seventeenth century, then careened and repaired; she was becalmed in the eighteenth century and, after steering a gusty course between the rocks of the Victorian era, she is now the oldest ship of a small fleet, tough and full of life in spite of her age, and sailing with a good wind, but needing again the shipwright's hand.'[1]

By the turn of 1550 the English Church had fallen on bad days. Its treasures had largely been filched and its mind was being clouded by a stream of Protestant immigrants who found England more hospitable than their continental home countries. The first Prayer Book, men decided, had made too many compromises with medievalism. Revision was called for. It came in 1552 accompanied

[1] *Everyman's History of the Prayer Book.*

by an Act of Uniformity which this time made it an offence for anyone to be absent from church on Sundays or Holy Days, while attendance at any other form of service became grounds for imprisonment.

The 1552 Book was an attempt to reverse the mind of its 1549 predecessor. As had happened before, Parliament took the law in its own hands without bothering to consult the ecclesiastical Convocations. And the notorious 'Black Rubric', denying any sort of real presence of our Lord in the Sacrament, was added. The second Prayer Book, indeed, was more a political gesture than an aid to spirituality. It lasted eight months and it had a lot to do with creating the enthusiasm with which the English greeted Mary when she succeeded Edward VI.

But Mary lit fires in Smithfield. And Prayer Books were prohibited. Her one desire was to restore the ancient order. It was like trying to put an hour-glass back after clocks had been invented. The whole period, but supremely the 1550s, was marred by violence and most of it centred around what men made of the King of Peace. But it stands as permanent evidence that the Church of England was not the whimsical fiat of a monarch who wanted a new wife but something carved in agony.

In 1558 began the Elizabethan age and within a year the 1559 Uniformity Act had liquidated the Marian legislation and restored the Prayer Book of 1552 with catholic modifications. The penalties for failing to use it were increased.

Elizabeth made it quite clear that she was answerable neither to Rome nor Geneva. But equally she was not going to be fanatically opposed to either. Thus was removed from the Litany the petition 'from the tyranny of the Bishop of Rome and all his detestable enormities, good Lord deliver us'. Thus was set part of the pattern of the Anglican mind ever since. It does not set out to criticise another Church but where it disagrees with another Church it sets out its own positive truth. The reaction of the bishops to the encyclical *Humanae Vitae* when they were assembled at the 1968 Lambeth Conference was a good example of this. Those Anglican bishops made no direct reference to the encyclical. They merely reiterated, in a positive manner, their own differing opinion as stated at a previous Lambeth Conference.

The sixteenth century Pope was not impressed by Elizabeth's action. In 1562 he launched his Bill of Excommunication against her and absolved all his followers from allegiance to England's Crown. It was a short-sighted move for it sent Roman Catholics out of English public life. At the same time the Puritan element was growing. They may have derived their theology from the continent but they owed no political allegiance to any foreign power. Accordingly they were able to attain high positions in the State. And soon they were making their minds clear. The 1559 Prayer Book, they said, was 'picked out of a Popish dunghill'. They had no room for bishops. They wanted to be rid of the Sign of the Cross in baptism and the ring in marriage. And they demanded a form of worship shorn of all externals. 'Because the Roman Catholic Church in common with the whole of Christendom up to the sixteenth century acted on the obvious truth that beauty is a good thing, the majority of Englishmen paid Rome the compliment of embracing ugliness for her sake' said Percy Dearmer. Again the Church of England was being subjected to an agony, but now from the inside. There were men who accepted office in it but showed no loyalty to it. There was no outward disobedience, no political dissension. Just an insidious maggot gnawing away.

Yet this was the period which produced great men like Hooker whose *Of the Laws of Ecclesiastical Polity*,[1] asserting the continuity of the Church of England with the whole of Catholic Christendom, is one of the greatest Anglican books ever written. And the Prayer Book was providing spiritual sustenance for giants like John Jewel, Lancelot Andrews, George Herbert, Jeremy Taylor and Margaret Godolphin.

But meanwhile, Puritan power was growing and it achieved its moment in 1644 when the Prayer Book was declared illegal – one of the grounds being that it was 'an offence to the Reformed Churches abroad'. And again there came the despoliation of churches with men like Will Dowsing being paid 8s. 6d. a time to

[1] R. Hooker, reissued by Scolar Press, 1969.

destroy ornaments–though in one place he was disgusted to get only 3s. 4d. because there were no more than 'ten superstitious pictures and a cross to be destroyed'. It was the time when, as Macaulay said 'men hated bear-baiting, not because it gave pain to the bear but because it gave pleasure to the spectators'.

Englishmen were ready for the Restoration. And Charles II tried to ensure that the Throne would henceforth remain inviolable by enforcing religious conformity. The Conventicle Act forbade meetings for worship where the Prayer Book was not used, the Licensing Act imposed a rigid Press censorship, the Five-Mile Act made nonconformist ministers wanderers in the wilderness, the Test Act insisted that all civil and military officers should take the oath of allegiance and receive the Holy Communion according to the Church of England rite. Charles was not concerned to legislate men into the kingdom of heaven. He just wanted to make sure that no one would deprive him of the kingdom of England.

There are so many points in the history of the Church of England where this part of the Body of Christ has been used for the oddest purposes. Other Churches have also not escaped a similar role. But the vicissitudes of the Church of England do prompt the reflection that any Church which lacked inner strength and truth must surely have disintegrated long since. The Church of England has survived despite Englishmen's doings. God must have a real reason for sustaining it.

Nine English bishops survived the Long Parliament and they expressed the grounds on which yet another Prayer Book revision should be made. The nearer they said, its forms 'come to the ancient liturgy of the Greek and Latin Churches, the less they are liable to the objections of the common enemy'.

Charles II had been back in London only a few months when he called a conference of all concerned to renew the Prayer Book. This Savoy Conference was a great battleground between the bishops and the very vocal Puritans–some of whom even wished to abolish the Lord's Prayer as a Popish invention. It is one of the mysteries that a conference called by a gay and unscrupulous king

D

to serve his own ends should have produced the Book of Common Prayer of 1662. Perhaps the reason lies in Charles's own disinterest in details. As long as he had a Prayer Book to focus national unity he was happy. Thus the Book was the fruit of the work of church-men who struggled to retain as far as they could a consensus of all the Christian centuries. True, the Book was appended to an Act of Uniformity and that makes it a legal document, part of the law of the land. Parliament accepted it but Parliament did not create it. That was left to the Church. Parliament could impose penalties on those who did not use it–the fate of someone who transgressed the Conventicle Act was transportation for life. But while that might hide the Book's intrinsic merit, it could not destroy it. The Church had emerged from a period of tribulation scarred but whole and it had its spiritual charter intact. At the time this Book was being formulated men were often more anxious vindictively to repay old injuries than to say their prayers and they were more inclined to compensate for Puritan rigidities in Restoration permissiveness than to live the Christian life. But the Spirit who guides the Church can use any occasion to his purpose and three centuries of Englishmen would come to thank God for the Book of Common Prayer.

And not only Englishmen. By 1551 the first translation had been made–into Latin, in the hope of inspiring continental reformers to follow suit. The first Welsh translation was in 1567 and Ireland followed in 1608. Frederick I of Prussia had a German version made in 1704 to try to heal the breach between Lutherans and Reformed in his domain. But the great majority of translations, now running into several hundreds, were made to accompany the growth of the Anglican Communion and nowadays Cranmer's phrases echo from northern igloos to southern palm-thatched huts.

But it was on the English that the Prayer Book had the greatest effect. Tired alike of Puritan fanaticism and Restoration follies they longed for the calm of a *via media*. In the half century follow-ing Charles II's return it soaked deep into the English soul. It has remained there ever since. And it has been a major factor in helping the Church of England to solve the problem of being at once a State Church and part of an ecumenical fellowship.

Yet such is the questing nature of Anglicanism, always aware that it is a pilgrim Church incessantly seeking something beyond itself, that the Prayer Book has never for long been left in peace. There have, for example, always been the tensions of those who have emphasised one element or the other of the Anglican synthesis and have used the Book selectively to express their convictions. And there have also always been more or less authoritative attempts at revision. The first came when the Prayer Book was only twenty-seven years old. The devotion of James II to Rome helped to bring closer relationships between Anglicans and Dissenters and this found expression in 1688 when Archbishop Sancroft set out to diminish the Prayer Book's catholic strands. The result earned the description 'a catena of almost intolerable verbosity' and it got lost in its own wordiness. William III also thought revision a good idea but this, too, got nowhere–though out of this situation came the Toleration Act of 1689, first sign of a move towards today's good relationships. To continue listing attempts at revision would be tedious–between 1751 and 1768 there were no less than six and the process continued. For Englishmen have always known that the Prayer Book is no magic formula guaranteed forever to ensure adequate worship but a human attempt to approach the Infinite One.

The Prayer Book has had a unique place. Yet to suggest that either leaders or the man in the pew have always been worthy of it is wrong. 'The Church of England as it now stands no human power can save' said Thomas Arnold in 1832. He was speaking on the eve of the unleashing of mighty forces. The turn of the nine-teenth century had seen the dawn of the splendour of the Evangeli-cal Revival, a significant renewal of personal devotion and religious fervour. The 1830s were to see the birth of the Oxford Movement with its great emphasis on catholicity and corporate worship. Increasingly it became clear that the Prayer Book could not con-tain the esoteric eccentricities to which this led. Before long the battle between the Rits (ritualists) and the Rats (rationalists) had reached scandalous proportions. In 1867 a Royal Commission was appointed to examine the situation. It did nothing to quell the combatants.

The last quarter of the nineteenth century was bespattered by internecine ecclesiastical warfare and it was total on both sides. Newspaper reporters had an orgy. In 1904 Parliament appointed a Select Committee and there began the story which ended with the rejection of the Revised Prayer Book by Parliament in 1927–8. In its first two years that Committee held 118 meetings and its report included 'the law of public worship in the Church of England is too narrow for the religious life of the present generation. . . . It is important that the law should be reformed, that it should admit of reasonable elasticity . . . above all, that it should be obeyed.'

Those last few words perhaps demonstrate why this attempt at reform failed. For the Committee was trying to create an instrument of discipline. For nearly a quarter of a century they argued and debated and drafted. Great public interest was aroused. And Parliament concluded this was no occasion for merely rubber-stamping what the Church seemed to want. The House of Lords gave the Revised Book its approval. But the Commons pontificated and, Anglican and non-Anglican, Christian and non-Christian, they solemnly voted against.

It is only too easy to write furious prose about a secular Parliament overruling the judgement of the Church on so intimate and spiritual a matter. It is also too facile. Had that 1928 Book gone through the matter would have been closed, probably for a century. Instead it has remained a live topic and sensitive to the vast liturgical thinking and ecumenical planning the last half-century has seen. We might have had a coelocanth. Instead we have a live, responsive species ready for mutation in much more favourable circumstances than the twenties could produce. Perhaps W. K. Lowther Clarke, writing in 1932, best summed it up: 'The many years of discussion have not been wasted. The English people have received an education in liturgical matters which otherwise would not have been possible. What seemed incredible actually came to pass. The holiest mysteries of the Faith were discussed in Parliament, but with such sincerity that cavilling was silenced. The controversy echoed round the world but some continental observers, at least, were not shocked but rather admired a country where the people were moved by matters of such a moment and said, "We envy you your controversies". The clash of Church and State, predicated by many, has not taken place. Much of the material collected by English scholars has found a place in Revised Prayer Books overseas. What seemed at the time a blow to the Church of England may wear a very different aspect in the eyes of future historians.'[1]

Over three centuries have elapsed since the present Book of Common Prayer was compiled. The English language has changed considerably. The use the State can make of the Church has changed even more. The relationships between members of the Church of England and other Christians have changed radically. The Book of Common Prayer of 1662 as authorised by the Act of Uniformity of that year still remains the only ultimately lawful authority. But Church and State have learned to live together on a happier basis. In 1966 there came into force the Prayer Book (Alternative and Other Services) Measure which sanctions variants for experimental use. The faithful are being asked to try new forms before Parliament is being asked to impose them as the law of the land. To produce these permissive forms, which to quite a large degree are recognitions of alternatives already–quite illegally–being used widely in churches, august bodies sat long and wearisomely. It is too early to say what the final outcome will be. Indeed, before that final outcome the relationship between Church and State may be very different and maybe Parliament will accept that prayer is more a matter for practising Christians than for politicians to decide. But there is one already obvious point–and it comes as a surprise to many people among whom the present writer admits he finds himself.

The logic of Prayer Book revision has long seemed quite irrefutable on a whole host of grounds. The need seemed so palpable that surely all would welcome it. That has by no means

[1] *Liturgy and Worship*, S.P.C.K., 1932, p. 790.

proved to be the case. Many a parish priest has found that the faithful deeply resent any changes in words or in forms which have grown familiar over a lifetime of devotion. Such resentment is not limited to any one class and, as the Roman Catholic Church has found over the Englishing of the Mass, very often it is the intellectuals and the aesthetes who most resent change. Maybe that is to be deplored. But it does point to public prayer and corporate worship as activities which go very deep into a man's nature and become part of himself. We are all conservatives at heart. There are undoubtedly many advantages about an ordered form of worship. But it does appear that there are times when order is a barrier to better order.

This chapter thus far has been something of a eulogy of the Prayer Book. What if the reader were someone who had never seen the Book and went along to his public library to borrow a copy? He might find it hard to share this author's enthusiasm for the Book. For although it is a Book, it was never really meant to be read. It will indeed stand up to reading and will yield much to the reader. But he will surely fail to grasp from a mere reading what it is all about. For the Book itself was never intended to be a compilation of ink, paper, print, binding and words held in the hand and perused. It was rather intended to be forgotten by its user as the soul rises in worship or receives the Holy Communion or the bride gives her vows to the bridegroom. Thus the experience of the Book in its proper public setting becomes something vital before it can be judged. That setting will include the presence of other people in a building designed for the purpose. Maybe the occasion will have all the pomp of a Winston Churchill funeral or maybe it will be a quiet, said service in a country church on a dark winter's morning. The precise setting does not matter but something with a high degree of familiarity is assumed. Even the first Prayer Book was not compiled for people who would never have heard its words before, nor would they be unfamiliar with the stones and decorations and atmosphere of some church to which they had long been accustomed. Such familiarity has its advantages, for the Prayer Book grows richer as it becomes daily better known.

But it also has its disadvantages, especially in a mobile society like our own for the man who moves house rarely finds it entirely easy to adjust to some different building. As clergy know so well, even to change the familiar tune for a hymn can cause offence. The hymns which form a minimal element in the services as they are set out, have acquired a major place in the minds and affections of most regular worshippers.

Understanding the Prayer Book properly demands familiarity with it. Yet the Book itself has built into it a considerable routine of change. For implicit in its structure and explicit in its use are the Church's seasons with their gay apparel of high moments like Christmas and Easter and their sombre hues of Lent or Advent. The Church has the capacity for always changing yet ever remaining the same and the Prayer Book articulates this.

We have spent much time on the corporate prayer of Anglicans in their day-by-day attendance at the regular ('statutory' is the usual word for them and it is revealing) services. The remarks we have made about them could, *mutatis mutandis*, be made about the 'occasional' services, that is, those designed to mark some special occasion. They, too, are part of the law of the land. When, for example, a clergyman solemnly signs a register saying that he has married someone 'according to the rites and ceremonies of the Church of England' he is the sole representative of the civil authority in attendance–other Churches have to resort to a Registrar–and he must abide by what that civil authority has approved as a valid ceremony.

The Anglican's spiritual life then, whether in regular services or on special occasions, is regulated for him and there are many consequent advantages. Yet they would be much emaciated were they not constantly being fed by a great stream of deep inner devotion. Anglicans talk of their 'incomparable Prayer Book'. They sometimes display an undue modesty (or could it be ignorance?) about Anglican spiritual writings.

We must again go back before the Reformation, and not least to the fourteenth century, when we consider Anglican spiritual writings. This was the day of *Piers Plowman* with his vision of the high tower of Truth in the deep dungeon of Wrong with the beggars, priests, lawyers and so on going about their business. Conscience does its preaching and Repentance moves hearts. But *Piers Plowman* is not concerned with spiritual things as matters of remote escapism. He is also absorbed in the social conditions of his day and labour problems get special attention as does the matter of corruption in the Church. *Piers Plowman* already establishes some of the primary characteristics of English spiritual writing. Thus, he is highly literary and is 'the most important work in Middle English with the exception of Chaucer's *Canterbury Tales*'.[1] To turn over the pages of a dictionary of quotations is to realise how much our language owes to spiritual writers. It is an illustration of the way that the English emphasis on the Incarnation, when God became flesh in his world, causes English religion to become part of the warp and woof of English life until we can no longer find a clear divide between sacred and secular.

Another effect of this incarnational thinking—and *Piers Plowman* illustrates this, too—is the way that English spiritual writing keeps its feet on the ground. Here is no escapism of saints from a world abdicated to sinners but rather a basic conviction that what God made is good and the place for Christians is in the middle of it.

Lest it be imagined that our reference to the medieval period rests on a single name, four others at least must be mentioned. Probably the greatest of all English mystics was Mother Julian of Norwich (born around 1342) who found in the divine love the clue to all existence and because of her conviction about it could assert 'All shall be well and all manner of thing shall be well'. Almost contemporary with her is Walter Hilton (died 1396) whose book, *Scala Perfectionis*[2] had vast influence. *The Cloud of Unknowing* has also been attributed to him. Among the people who influenced him was Richard Rolle (*c*. 1295–1349) one of the first religious authors to write in the vernacular. There is also Margery Kempe, born around 1373, whose life and writings stimulate fascinating thoughts about medieval religion.

[1] *Oxford Companion to English Literature*, Oxford University Press, 1967.
[2] *The Scale of Perfection*, reissued by Burns & Oates, 1953.

The story goes on through men like John Colet (*c.* 1466–1519), John Foxe (1516–87) (*The Book of Martyrs* was published in 1563 when memories of Mary's reign were still warm), John Donne (*c.* 1573–1631), George Herbert (1593–1633), Sir Thomas Browne (1605–82) and continues to our day (the words chosen to head this chapter were written by a Dean of York only recently dead). The list is a familiar one and is part of the heritage of any cultured Englishman. One reason for that is because the English clergy were never trained in any remote seminaries but took their place with their compatriots at the usual universities. Indeed, until the nineteenth century there were no theological colleges as such. English spiritual writing, accordingly, has a robustness which marches into all the byways. When Hemingway wanted a title for a novel he went to John Donne and found a passage which includes words which so utterly describe the twentieth-century human condition – 'No man is an island' – that they have become the common property of all men. Donne, a clergyman, did not set out just to make men 'holy' in any sanctuary-limited sense but to make men think. The Anglican emphasis on the right and duty of each man to use his common sense is a leit-motif of Anglican spiritual writing. A consequence of this emphasis is that any raw material of thought from any source deserves examination. Anglicans have never been confined by an Index of prohibited writings and their devotional manuals have been catholic in its widest sense. They have a powerful precedent, for Paul did not scorn to quote 'your own poets' when he spoke to the men of Athens. The prayers of East and West and the dreams of Plato and Plotinus have all been grist to an English mill.

Perhaps it is this universality of choice combined with some phlegm of the English character which have helped Anglican spiritual writings to hold a balance between reason and emotion. Not, of course, that each individual has in himself been able to harmonise this tension. There have always been the 'enthusiastic' whose ardent zeal has led them into mawkish orgies and there have always been the cold logicians who treat theology like a theorem. But range over the centuries and balance is your reward.

43

Reason always comes up somewhere in the picture while feeling is there to make it human. Tradition comes in to give them substance and overarching them all is a deep faith which accepts their validity and then soars beyond them. Maybe the *tout ensemble* has resulted in sermons less likely to produce compulsive response than the more colourful rantings of a popular preacher. But you cannot have everything and Anglicanism, convinced that its Lord wanted to lead men, not to drag and dragoon them, has opted to address itself to reason, conscience and experience and leave the more powerful emotional opiates to others. No doubt Anglicanism's insistence on the Bible as the anchor has much to do with this. No doubt the Anglican conviction that the feelings and thoughts induced in the sanctuary have to be worked out in the market place is another factor. ('The Church of England has, at its best, given superb expression to a full range of experiences and needs' said Marghanita Laski.)[1] And without question the possession of a Book of Common Prayer, as much the property of the man in the pew as of his priest, has made a vital contribution to it all. Any Anglican spiritual writing is done on the assumption that it speaks to people familiar with this Prayer Book and it must be judged by the standards of this book. Having this Book, Anglicans have felt little called to produce complex treatises on the more exotic intricacies of devotion. Instead they assume that devotion is going to be a natural, homespun thing. They are more interested in praying than describing methods of prayer. Lacking high drama it may seem a little dull to the outsider. But then, the onlooker never does finally appreciate the feeling of the game. Anglican devotion has succeeded in being meaningful for the tyro and has also satisfied souls in their most advanced journeyings. Underlying it all is the idea that God is near (for this is incarnational religion) and our approach to him must be natural. Anglicanism has not been made neurotic by extreme overtones of human depravity nor has it become casual through extreme confidence in the efficacy of human works. Instead it can say 'Our Father' knowing a father as one who deserves final respect and yet always remains approachable.

[1] *Punch*, 23 June 1965.

They also know that sonship is a matter of experience rather than a fruit of theorising. As a result Anglican spiritual writings are not much concerned with speculation on the mysteries of the Faith. They do not tie themselves in knots about the mechanics of *how* Christ is present in the Blessed Sacrament but rather they give thanks for the fact that he is. They would, so to speak, rather enjoy a rose than analyse its substance and attributes.

It can – and indeed it does – all add up to an impression of English casualness in religion and many are the aphorisms as a result ('The Church of England give you a touch of religion to save you from the real thing' is an example). Yet the consensus of English devotional writing speaks differently. The preparation for the approach to God, whether in his sacrament or anywhere else, is in the whole of life not in some precise set of words immediately beforehand. That can make the Anglican careless about formulae and casual about church-going but it also teaches him that the Christian faith is a total call to us to be total men. There is no doubt about man's duty to join with his fellows in worshipping God. But Anglican devotional writing also makes it clear that there is no doubt that church-going by itself is not enough. The duty to God and the duty towards one's neighbour are insistently held together and the consequence is a duty to live one's whole life *sub specie aeternitatis* with attention to the Eternal having its focal points in the now of public worship.

The one person above all whom a Church of England clergyman finds hard to help is the man who says, 'Give me the detailed rules about churchgoing, Bible-reading, prayer, almsgiving, works of mercy, etc., etc., and I will fulfil them.' There is no set answer. Maybe it is a pity, for such a man usually comes because he has lost security and confidence and he is seeking crutches to help him get along. The Church of England can only remember that its Lord said 'Get up. Pick up your bed. Walk on your own feet.' He also said, 'Thy faith hath made thee whole.' Wholeness is something towards which the Church of England still has to struggle. But there are grounds for believing that the direction in which this Church is set is the right one.

45

3

The Past is Prologue

'The happiest women, like the happiest nations, have no history', said George Eliot in *The Mill on the Floss*. The same might be said of Churches.

It is an axiom of Fleet Street that the norm is not news. It is the things which stick out that get reported. Since history is the catena of the news that managed to survive it must be subject to the same laws. He who reads the story of the Church on earth must expect to be fully informed about the abnormalities, and not least those which were a source of scandal. That such scandals do occur is no more than evidence that the work of the Church as a channel of grace and the gateway to glory remains eternally unfinished in the human sphere. Each new infant born is a new challenge to the Church. It is those who make mistakes, whether wearing mitres or crowns or cloth caps, who are remembered. What is constantly forgotten is that the Church has prevailed over two millenia because basically its human end consists of a myriad holy souls who generation by generation have said their prayers and done godly things and avoided sensational headlines. They were not 'kings thirty feet high'. They were kneeling, so they attracted little attention. We must leave them at their orisons as we review the record of a body committed to the tension of making real the sacred in the midst of the secular. Let this chapter be read, then, in the knowledge that while what it says, as far as one can achieve it, is true, it leaves a greater truth unsaid.

What are the origins of the Church of England? He who is challenged to answer such a question can only begin by asking another: what are the origins of the English people? We can only be brief.

Before history was recorded, immigrants began to come to this

46

country from the Mediterranean by two routes: by sea, around Gibraltar and up the western coasts for minerals like lead and gold; and by land across the continent and by ferry across the channel. In the early centuries of our era it was the latter which became identified with the Roman invasion but the first never really ceased.

When the Christian message began to burgeon in the Middle East it had these two highways available. The traders who gossipped with the miners about the God who had died and risen again were one source of information. Tradition, drawing a very long but not entirely impossible bow, suggests they may have included Joseph of Arimathaea and even the boy Jesus might have been brought here for the ride. The other source was the Roman armies with their diverse camp followers. The Roman soldier who stood at the foot of the Cross and became one of the first Christians when he said 'Truly this man is the Son of God' might have ended his days in Britain. There is also a tradition, attractive but unsubstantiated, that Paul the Apostle preached in London.

What is quite certain is that Christianity in Britain did not begin with any organised mission nor did it initially have sufficient identity for one to say 'At that moment the Church began here'. Instead, here a little and there a little—and probably very patchily in different parts of Britain—the Church of England began. Obviously such an event, even had it been recognised as news, would hardly be bruited abroad. In a Roman Empire given to periods of persecution it would not be expedient to keep records even if anyone had thought of doing so. Nor, again, would Christians think it wise to build special places of worship. Mithras, who could come to terms with Emperor worship, could have his Temple in the middle of Roman London. Christians, who could give Crown Rights only to their Redeemer, would more probably have used a housechurch on a site outside the walls like the one where St Bride's, Fleet Street, stands today. What does seem certain is that the more the archaeologists dig the more they reveal of Christian possibilities in days not too many decades removed from the Resurrection.

The first written mention of Christians in Britain is by Tertullian around the year 208. The fact that he lived most of his life in North Africa meant that news of the British Christians had spread far. More interesting, however, as evidence of Christianity arriving here by non-Roman paths, is his statement that parts of Britain inaccessible to Romans had already been conquered by Christ. Thirty years later Origen, who was born in Egypt and spent most of his life in the eastern Mediterranean, was also noting the presence of Christians in Britain. Britain's first recorded martyr is associated with the Diocletian persecution of A.D. 305 and by 314 Britain was able to send three bishops to the Council of Arles while in 360 another three bishops were present at the Council of Ariminum–though they were so poor that they had to depend on the government for their travelling expenses.

The picture then, is of a fairly lively Church in England in Romano-British times. Whence then the suggestion that Augustine arrived to face a pagan situation in 597 ? The answer lies with the Angles, Saxons and Jutes. As the Roman legions departed, the country was left exposed. Coming from their continental forests they knew nothing about the Prince of Peace nor did they know about urban settlements. They broke up what they found and Christians were driven westward, into Welsh and Irish fastnesses, and northwards. In time those areas were to send missionaries to Europe but for the moment they were to develop the culture which was a glorious Celtic sunset. Their Christianity, like their civilisation, did not centre on cities and therefore developed no prestigious organisation. Nor did it acquire the cohesion which would enable it to challenge the more highly organised Roman system when Augustine brought it to these shores. But even Augustine did not write it off. When he arrived he found that Bertha, wife of King Ethelbert, was already a Christian and when he wrote to Rome about the Christian vestiges he found even in Kent, Pope Gregory's famous reply told him not to destroy what he found nor to impose upon it all the customs with which he had become familiar in Rome. Thus did Rome recognise the validity of Celtic Christianity.

Britain, accordingly, had two main streams of Christianity–

Celtic and Roman—or three, if the Romano-British deserves separate mention. Apart from the incursions of the Danes its growth was henceforward to be steady. But it was also to be a tension. The flowery Celt and the austere Roman were to have many differences. But it is erroneous to think of Roman and Celt as seeing themselves belonging to different Churches. Rather they owed loyalty to one Church only but held that local circumstances had given rise to a variety of local customs—like the Celtic remoteness of Iona or Lindisfarne or Kildare giving rise to a looser monastic system than that of the highly organised urban stream of Rome.

It was in 663, at the Synod of Whitby, that the confluence came. The debate was over details like the date of Easter and the way the clergy cut their hair. The real argument was, as it is today, about the nature of authority. The Roman stream, with all the weight of *imperium* behind it, won the day and for nine centuries England's Church was to be linked with the Bishop of Rome—to call him Pope at this stage would be a misleading anachronism. The continuing tension was to be between variety and uniformity, between independence and centralisation. It was a tension not much felt in the initial stages, for Rome itself had not then developed the authoritarianism which was its mark from the Middle Ages to Vatican II. And it was a tension which had its totally non-theological factors—such as the Norman Conquest which for four centuries was to make England unquestionably part of Europe.

It was seven years after the Norman Conquest that, in 1073, the magnificent Hildebrand became Pope. His zeal for righteousness led him to insist that kings had to be made subservient to the Church and spiritual rulers had to be supreme in all things. William the Conqueror, though he had special reasons for being grateful to the Pope, would have none of that. He flatly refused to give fealty to Hildebrand. He forbade papal letters to be received in England without his permission nor did he let English bishops go to Rome for any reason or on any grounds, spiritual or otherwise, until they had his permission. Thus there grew up what were known as the 'ancestral customs' of England which were to mean that Henry VIII did not have to invent anything new but was able to restate and crystallise a position honoured by centuries. Not least of these customs was the right of the English monarch to nominate the bishop–in language of high political double-talk. 'I order you to hold a free election, but, nevertheless, I forbid you to elect anyone except Richard, my clerk', wrote Henry II to the monks of Winchester in the year that Thomas à Becket was canonised. This *congé d'élire* (permission to elect) still goes to cathedral chapters when a bishop is to be chosen and its use, in one form or another, long predates the Conqueror. But then, so do so many other facets of this Church of England. What is quite certain–and is of basic importance–is that the Church of England was an entity before there was a nation of England. With a country divided into so many tribal kingdoms this Church provided a unity which was vital. An archbishop could provide an emotional as well as an actual centre long before any king could. This had a more than ecclesiastical significance. Speaking of this Church, Bishop J.W.C.Wand says: 'It is important in secular history inasmuch as it enabled England to realise the ideal of national unity earlier than any of the continental countries.'[1]

This idea of the Church as a centre of national unity and a means of national identity comes strange to modern Englishmen so it is worth a diversion to look at what is probably the most striking example of all. A few years ago many people wondered how Archbishop Makarios had the time, the authority or the inclination to be so politically active. Christianity was founded in Cyprus by Paul and Barnabas. When the Arabs took over the island, the Christian Faith became the symbol of the people's opposition to their conquerors. When they got rid of the Arabs in the tenth century there followed four centuries of violent strife between the Greek and the Latin Churches, thus keeping religion a very live issue. When the Turks took over in 1571, the Latin Church was exterminated and the Greek remnant, though persecuted, survived to become the focal point of Greekness against the Turkish overlords. All this has been distilled into loyalty to the leader of

[1] *Anglicanism in History and Today*, Weidenfeld & Nicolson, 1961.

the Greek Church as a figurehead. He is accordingly entrusted with political as well as spiritual authority.

'Go amongst the Greeks, the Russians, the Armenians and the rest', said the great historian, Adolf Harnack, 'and you will everywhere find that religion and nationality are inseparable and the one element exists only in and alongside the other.' Good Friday in Athens, with flags on public buildings at half-mast and police bands playing the *Dead March* illustrates the point. Religion and life are not the disparates the secularist would have us believe.

The English Church played a vital part in England's secular history. It is this fact which helps modern man to understand a situation so different from the one he knows. In the Middle Ages, bishops were great nobles and the country's leading administrators. And in those days, not a few of the English bishops would spend most of their lives in Rome, a system the English King found useful for it gave him agents to keep an eye on his rival power. And holders of English ecclesiastical office could also hold posts in Spain or Belgium or elsewhere while Spaniards and the rest could have titular office in England without even visiting the place. All of which meant that their English duties had to be fulfilled by impecunious clerks-'vicars'-who did not necessarily have either the best qualifications or the greatest zeal. Even had there been no other failings, this alone would have been enough to make the ordinary Englishman feel that his Church needed reformation.

There were many signs that a break with Rome was coming. In 1236 the Council of London barred the papal delegate from its discussions. In 1281 Bishop Peckham was publicly asserting that England had its own individual religious life and it had to maintain this. In 1377 the Commons insisted that the clergy-and therefore Rome-had no right to make statutes without their consent. In 1351, 1353, 1365 and 1389 various Statutes of Provisors were passed with the object of depriving the Pope of any influence in important appointments to English benefices. In 1353 the first statute of Praemunire did much to diminish the powers of papal courts.

England, in fact, was never really a part of the Holy Roman

Empire. It was never, for example, included in the areas where the Inquisition operated. And as early as Henry V, the English king exercised the right to suppress foreign monasteries in England even though they were under the special protection of the papacy. When the spirit of nationalism began to grow, England had a good start on most of the continental countries which may be one reason why the change had less disrupting effect. And for England, national identity was an impossibility if her Church were controlled by some foreign authority, for that Church was so well endowed with resources of men and materials. It has been estimated that as much as one-third of the whole land surface of England was ecclesiasical property in one form or another while as much as two per cent of the adult male population were probably clerics of some degree. The Church's holy days were the community holidays. Every village had its parson and little could happen without him knowing. Excommunication was an ever ready weapon depriving men of civil as well as spiritual rights. All power corrupts, and the human beings who exercised such authority in medieval England had no guaranteed immunity. Vast numbers of them were holy souls. But there were enough of the other sort to provide grounds for insistence on reform. Even if, however, all the clerics and nuns had been paragons, the Church had gone sadly astray. For this bejewelled medieval fortress bore little resemblance to its Master who was men's servant. He who had had nowhere to lay his head was a prisoner of magnificence. It was little wonder that an illiterate population sank into superstition. And that very superstition, convinced that handing one's wealth to the Church brought salvation, fed its own sources and grew more ugly. Like having two, and even three, Popes at the same time, each claiming full allegiance and impugning his rivals. Even so, there still flowed in England a deep stream of spirituality as was shown by the reference to religious writings in the last chapter.

There also flowed, throughout Europe, the liberating flood of the Renaissance. To many of the Churchmen of the day it must have looked like the end of Christendom and like other points in history it compels the questions: why does God choose to renew his

Church by forces outside the Church, why is it that the secular so often brings new life to the sacred ?

We have not time here to pursue such attractive thoughts. We must look at the Reformation which in England took a unique form. In the first place it insisted on the maximum amount of continuity with the past without perpetuating its errors. In the second place, it asserted Britain's national independence of any foreign power, political or spiritual. Thirdly it subordinated Church to State. In a sense, however, the second and third of those points are derivatives of the first. The nationalism of the English was no new feature of their character. They had always been an insular people and they were reasserting it. And the subordination of the Church to the State could also find roots as far back as Constantine while one English monarch after another, from the Conqueror on, had played a large part in the selection of the Church's senior officers and therefore the shaping of the Church's policy.

These were powerful forces and when there was added to them the spiritual dynamism which was the longing for religious freedom across Europe, it becomes evident that Henry VIII's matrimonial habits were merely an occasion and not a cause. It was ironic that the occasion should be a man of high theological achievement, one who had fully earned from the Pope the title of Defender of the Faith. Yet it was also significant, for it meant that here was a man who would ensure that the break was only with the Pope and not with the Catholic Faith.

Right in front of Henry's eyes was a cardinal who had proved that a single man could hold in his own hands the highest powers in Church and State. If Wolsey could wield secular as well as ecclesiatical power then Henry, 'the Lord's anointed' by virtue of his coronation, could head the Church as well as the State.

Henry strove to maintain continuity. But he had breached a dam. And powerful men in the reign of Henry's weak successor were determined to let the floods wash all former things away. Their day was short and then came Mary. Ironically, she was as ruthless as any monarch in her assertion of royal supremacy over the Church. But she ill-served what she loved best. She did succeed in stifling the extremes of continental Protestanism. But her methods made papalism more than ever alien to the English people. If ever this country had been 'Roman Catholic' in the full sense of those words – and it can be argued that such had not been the case – Mary ensured that it could never be so again. The mood which was to defeat the Spanish armada had been created.

From Mary to Elizabeth. Much paper has been taken up with the complexity of her character and the ramifications of her motives. But one thing may be safely said. She intended to be Queen of England. The first task, therefore, was to secure a unified country and English religion lay at the heart of this. The raw material she had to work on consisted of a chaos of thought and a confusion of activities consequent upon the sudden changes between Protestant power under Edward VI and Roman Catholic revenge under Mary. But the great majority of the English were not extreme papists nor zealot reformers. Elizabeth's Prayer Book of 1559, the support of the moderate Archbishop Parker, and the common man's desire for peace, enabled her to lead England's most exciting half-century. The Roman Catholics themselves helped much to consolidate her position. When Pope Pius excommunicated her in 1570 and even more when the Spanish Armada came in 1588 to challenge the Englishman's peace, they were making a real contribution to Anglican solidarity. Englishmen became assured of their superiority over foreigners and therefore over foreign religions whether extreme Catholic or extreme Protestant.

The lineaments of the Church of England had been drawn. They were distinctive not in terms of any particular element, for they contained nothing that no other Church possessed, but rather in their balance. Balance, however, is a precarious thing and it demands constant effort to maintain it. The last three and a half centuries of the Church of England have been a dialectic of Christendom. The disputatiousness of the exponents of one extreme or the other has somehow been held if not in harmony at least in the same orchestra. 'Creative tension' is a cliché yet it has meaning and for the Church of England there seems no better phrase. But the outsider–and sometimes, too, the insider–must be forgiven if he finds it baffling.

Elizabeth herself felt those opposing forces and so did her successor. James I had hardly ascended the throne when he was approached by a powerful group of Protestants petitioning the deletion of much of the Prayer Book. The result was the Hampton Court Conference which resulted in insignificant changes in the liturgy but the most influential English translation of the Bible ever made. The 'Authorised' Version (it was never officially authorised) took two years and nine months to prepare and the first edition appeared in 1611 and cost 30s. bound. And again there is the quest for continuity, for those who worked on it insisted it was a revision, not a new translation.

Meanwhile Protestant power continued to grow and in due course there came the Long Parliament and the last great upheaval of both Crown and Church. The Protestants had a major opportunity of showing that they could commend themselves to the English people as leaders of their spiritual pilgrimage. They failed: and the Restoration was as significant a rejection of undiluted Protestantism as Henry VIII's dismissal of the Pope had been a rejection of Roman Catholicism. From this time on the Church of England would remain the Church of England–not a little helped by the fact that the dawn and growth of toleration enabled extremists to hive off on their own and thus deprived them of their greatest reason for staying inside the Church of England and battling to change its character. An interesting thing over the years has been just how many of these extremists have chosen to maintain a loyalty to the See of Canterbury and at the same time go on struggling to achieve their ideals. The most recent manifestation of this was in the long discussions about Anglican-Methodist unity. The parties inside the Church of England rallied themselves around two clear points, one Catholic and one Protestant.

This is a book about the Church of England. Yet it must remain incomplete and unbalanced if we omit a glance at the Anglican Communion. In any case, to study the Anglican Communion is to see the Church of England and its sister Churches in Wales, Scotland and Ireland writ large and therefore, perhaps, more clearly to see its nature.

Seeley's famous remark that 'We (the English) seem, as it were, to have conquered and peopled half the world in a fit of absence of mind' is even more true about the Anglican Communion. Not only did England and her Church never deliberately set out to create a worldwide Communion: there were also so many points at which both Church and State seemed actively to oppose the possibility. One perhaps natural but nevertheless false assumption can immediately be dismissed. The Anglican Communion is not a prayerful derivative of the British Empire. This Communion extends where the Empire never touched – Japan, Korea, Madagascar, Iran, Latin America, for example – and there were times when empire builders fiercely resented its presence. To name but one: when the East India Company got its Charter in 1600 its servants were clearly told that they must not interfere with the religion of the people among whom they worked. Even the Company chaplains had their activities severely restricted to the spiritual needs of the Company's expatriate staff. As late as Queen Victoria we get the same mood. When she assumed her title of Empress of India she declared 'We do strictly charge and enjoin all those who may be in authority under us that they abstain from all interference with the religious belief or worship of any of our subjects on pain of our highest displeasure.'

When countries like Spain and Portugal embarked on world empire they made it clear that the extension of Christianity was as much a duty as the extension of territorial power. The nearest that England could get to letting her Faith be practised overseas in the early years of her expansion was to enjoin that every ship over 500 tons burthen should carry a chaplain – and a remarkable number seemed to be 499 tons or less. However, the result was that as early as 1553 a service was probably held in Russia during Willoughby and Chancellor's voyage in search of a north-east passage to Cathay while in 1578 the Holy Communion according to the English Prayer Book was celebrated on the shores of Hudson Bay and the following year Sir Francis Drake's chaplain held a service in the presence of a large number of Red Indians. The first recorded baptism in America was Virginia Dare (of parents married in St Bride's, Fleet Street) in 1587. By 1607 the first colonial chaplain was appointed in America. But this promising start was not followed up. In fact, the Church of England in any official capacity would not follow it up for nearly two centuries. Missionary expansion, instead, was left to voluntary agencies who had to depend on their own capacities to find resources of men and money for the work. By 1674, when there were already many Englishmen abroad and they were, as far as officialdom was concerned, spiritual orphans, a Royal Commission had decided that the spiritual needs and ecclesiastical organisation of any remote Englishmen anywhere in the world were the responsibility of the Bishop of London because of his connection with the chief seaport. By then the spiritual state of colonists had reached a low ebb and observers said that their morals were hardly distinguishable from those of the Red Indians and black slaves among them they lived. It was Henry Compton who as Bishop of London took the first significant steps and his efforts resulted in the Society for Promoting Christian Knowledge in 1698, charged to send books to settlers, and the Society for the Propagation of the Gospel in 1701, charged to send living agents. There then followed the saddening spectacle of a Church and State which insisted that bishops were necessary for the proper life of the Church in England refusing to send bishops to a Church its voluntary agencies were building overseas. At one time the Church would make vast efforts to do so and find the State unwilling, and at other both Church and State would be willing but would lose nerve in the face of opposition from colonists who maintained they had left England to escape episcopacy. The history of Anglican work in America in the first three quarters of the eighteenth century is a strange compound of magnificent heroism – one in five of missionaries were lost at sea and practically all of them faced daunting odds – and a lamentable unawareness of authorities at home about what was actually happening. W. F. France writes: 'The narrative is at once amazing and shameful.

The Society for the Propagation of the Gospel at first tried to persuade the Law Officers of the Crown that Suffragan Bishops might properly be appointed; next it won the approval of Queen Anne, only to be defeated by her death; then it had the matter raised in Convocation, but the conspicuous absence of the Bishop of London (who felt his jurisdiction was thereby being diminished) prevented discussion and soon afterwards Convocation ceased. The Society then once again approached the Throne and it was strongly backed by Archbishop Tennison and his successors. It received large gifts for episcopal endowment from the Archbishop, from a Governor in Virginia, and others; it was strengthened by repeated memorials from statesmen and humble settlers in the colonies. But always political opposition was too powerful.'

The position was not to improve until 'the loss of the first British Empire' (two thirds of those who signed the American Declaration of Independence were Anglicans). America thus freed from Crown interference, could make her own plans about a bishop and she lost no time. Among the Americans who supported the call for a bishop were Benjamin Franklin and George Washington (who immediately after his swearing in as President went across the road to a church and received Holy Communion as an Anglican). In 1783 fourteen Connecticut clergy elected Samuel Seabury as their first bishop. But he still had to be consecrated and even here the dismal story continues. Seabury came to Lambeth and its archbishop dithered. If he consecrated Seabury would he be giving comfort to the King's enemies? And could a man receive Anglican consecration if he did not take an oath of loyalty to the Crown? And did it imply continuing English interference in American affairs? The Archbishop had no doubt that Anglicans in America needed a bishop lest their Church die of inanition. But he was an Englishman as well as an archbishop. It was Seabury himself who cut the Gordian knot. He remembered that the bishops of the Episcopal Church in Soctland had refused the Oath of Allegiance to the English Crown–in fact, as far as the English Crown was concerned there just were not any bishops in Scotland:

that was a Calvinist, Presbyterian preserve. But spiritual needs, even in the British Isles, can outweigh political formulae and in 1784 three Scottish bishops consecrated the first Anglican bishop who was not a member of the Church of England. That such a thing was even conceivable might have been something of a shock to England but it soon recovered its poise. In 1786 George III signed an Act which permitted English bishops to consecrate 'persons who are subjects or citizens of countries outside of His Majesty's dominions' and the way was open. Two American bishops, consecrated in Lambeth Palace chapel (with the then American Ambassador present) in 1787 were the harbingers of the several hundred Anglican but not English bishops scattered round the world today. Canada was next with its first Anglican bishop in 1787, India in 1814, the West Indies in 1824 and Australia in 1836. Two years later was passed an Act allowing the appointment of overseas bishops without first consulting the Crown. One of the first fruits of this was the Jerusalem bishopric in 1841, the first in a country where England had no political sway.

This bishopric provides an interesting study in the Church of England's capacity for acquiring unlikely relationships. The scheme was intended to serve both expatriate Anglicans in the Holy Land and also various Protestant groups. Accordingly it provided that the appointment of the bishop should alternate between England and Prussia, an arrangement which had little appeal either for the non-episcopal Lutherans or for the High Church Anglicans who saw in it an insidious alliance with a Protestant body with little hope of preserving Anglican order. It was not long, however, before the Prussians dropped out and since 1886 the bishopric has been wholly maintained by Anglicans. Another somewhat improbable aspect of it was that the first bishop, M. S. Alexander, was a convert from orthodox Judaism.

It was a period of great activity in the Church of England both at home and in its overseas work (which continued to be organised voluntarily rather than officially). Indeed 'the nineteenth century witnessed a striking awakening and transformation within the Church of England. In a sense the real reformation in that Church

59

was then rather than in the sixteenth and seventeenth centuries'[1] says the distinguished Kenneth Scott Latourette. The new life had come from both wings of the Church. The great Evangelical Revival which had marked the turn of the nineteenth century was followed by the Oxford Movement which began in a protest against State interference with the life of the Church and developed into a vigorous recrudescence of all that was Catholic. Strangely, it was a period when the Church had no corporate voice of any sort. In 1717 the Convocations of Canterbury and York had been prorogued by Royal Writ (Canterbury Convocation boldly recommenced in 1852 and York in 1861) and the Church was a long way from its twentieth-century organisation. Yet the Church was growing, and especially overseas. Lest the reader suspect, however, that there was some imperial urge in Britain which stimulated ecclesiastical expansion, let him remember how much Britons at the time were complaining at the cost of the colonies and Lord Grey's remark in 1848, 'There begins to prevail an opinion that we have no interest in preserving our colonies and ought therefore to make no sacrifice for that purpose.' 'The Church,' says Canon McLeod Campbell, 'so far from being carried on a rising tide of imperial ardour, had to battle against prevailing tendencies that discouraged if they did not discountenance overseas adventure.'[2]

What caused the growth of the Anglican Communion was not the English State but the deep conviction inside the minds of Churchmen that mission was a duty laid upon his followers by Christ himself. Its motive was spiritual and it was powerful. It also annihilated the idea that the Church of England could do only what the kingdom of England thought expedient. Whereas earlier bishops had been consecrated in Lambeth Palace chapel secretly like clandestine conspirators, in 1837 four bishops were consecrated in Westminster Abbey and Anglican growth moved from being a dubious exercise for eccentrics to an honoured undertaking.

It is of the providence of God that that growth should produce

---

[1] *A History of Christianity*, Eyre and Spottiswoode, 1954.
[2] *Christian History in the Making*, Press and Publications Board of the Church Assembly, 1946.

problems which forced the Church to look deep into its heart. Not least of these ranged round the name of the great but problematic John William Colenso. An algebraist of fame (author of a book which haunted schoolboys for generations), in 1853 he moved from his classroom to become Bishop of Natal. Colenso's heart was as big as his mathematical brain and before long compassion was stimulating him to ride lightly to Church law in matters such as polygamy among the Africans. He had also published some Bible commentaries which seriously fluttered the dovecotes. It was an age of savage controversy about religion, both within the Church from *avant-garde* theologians and from outside from peoples' interpretation of what Darwin had done to the Book of Genesis. Colenso was, it appeared, giving comfort to the Church's enemies. Robert Gray, his senior bishop in South Africa, felt compelled to act. Supported by forty-one English bishops, Gray asked Colenso to resign his see. Colenso refused. A trial was set up in Cape Town and it deposed Colenso. Colenso refused to recognise its competence and insisted only the Crown could remove him–though the Crown had had no hand in his appointment. Gray insisted that although the Church in South Africa 'is bound by and claims as its inherit-ance the standards and formularies of the Church of England, it is not bound by any interpretations put upon those standards by existing ecclesiastical courts in England or by any decision of such courts in matters of faith'. Here was a clear announcement that the Church of England and the constitutional complexities in which it found itself were not the same thing. Slowly the Church was coming to realise that the shackles of centuries need not be eternal.

Colenso illustrates so much in the life of the Church of England. The appointment of this great mathematical brain combined with real Christian devotion to a bishopric with intricate problems and needing a man of experience to lay down precedents betrayed England's conviction that anyone could be a bishop if he was reasonably educated and a gentleman. The controversy showed that there was more to Church leadership than that.

Colenso's story throws light upon episcopacy. But it also

accentuated another matter which Anglicans had never previously considered. Whatever England might make of its connections with an authority over the Church in South Africa was vital to other parts of Anglican missionary venture. In 1865 the Provincial Synod of the Church in Canada wondered just where it stood in relation to the English State. And so they wrote to the Archbishop of Canterbury asking for 'a Council of all the bishops in communion with your Grace'. Canada found ready support in America whose Anglican bishops had been invited for the first time to visit England in 1851 and had enjoyed the experience and wanted to build it up.

Thus from the periphery to the centre came the request: let the leaders of the Church meet to pray and talk about the life of the Church.

One would expect the answer to be an obvious Yes in all quarters. But not so. Those Englishmen–and there were many of them– who followed the doctrines of Erastus and insisted that the State was by nature always supreme in ecclesiastical matters went round like roaring lions seeking whom they might devour. Ardent Englishmen shuddered at the impudence of colonies making demands on their mother and zealous Protestants shivered at the thought of bishops ganging-up to concoct dark Catholic schemes.

The Archbishop of Canterbury of the day was known as a mild and amiable man. But he also saw the real need which existed. Accordingly he found a formula which might again be described as an Anglican compromise but which also underlines the wisdom that can lie in the middle way. A Council, he said, was impossible, for that implied a body which would make laws and lay down rules and bishops on their own were not competent to do that. It was a matter for the whole Church. But, on the other hand, there was much to be said for all the bishops meeting for 'brotherly consultations . . . united worship and common counsels would greatly tend to maintain practically the unity of faith'. Thus occurred the first Lambeth Conference.

Of the 144 invitations, 76 were accepted. But there were significant absentees. The Archbishop of York and all the northern bishops refused to attend. And the famous Dean Stanley of West-minster absolutely forbade the use of the Abbey for the closing service of thanksgiving. The sanction of 'a church so venerable and national in character' could not be bestowed upon bishops who might decide there was something bigger than the nation.

That first Lambeth Conference was held in 1867 and it has now had nine successors. The tone set in the original has been main-tained and the Conference claims no authority beyond its own prestige. It passes Resolutions but they are merely the opinion of the bishops until they have been accepted by the various Churches of this Anglican Communion—and history has shown that these Churches are far from rubber stamps when the Lambeth resolu-tions are being considered by their own authorised bodies. Thus a Lambeth decision can be rejected by the Church of England or by the Province of the West Indies or anywhere else.

Perhaps this is the point where we can best see one of Anglican-ism's greatest longings, to marry freedom and authority. There are Churches—and they can be found at both ends of the theological spectrum—where authority has rigidly prescribed every detail and the average member is allowed neither room for decision nor the chance to grow up. There are Churches which have experi-mented with utter freedom, where each member moves at each moment just as the Spirit seems to prompt him but they have not lasted long without adopting some sort of order or at least orderliness. From the tiniest village church to the structure of the whole Comm-union there is in Anglicanism the underlying urge to do nothing which inhibits the freedom of any individual but at the same time to do all that is possible for the smooth working of the body as a whole. The image of Anglicanism as a sort of ecclesiastical mudd-ling though is false for there is much more authority in this Church than most people imagine. Yet at the same time it is an authority which, so to speak, is never used. The analogy of marriage is often used. Bride and bridegroom accept the authority of their marriage vows and at the same time the full freedom to belong that those vows give. Each, in marrying, gives away freedom and yet receives a new and greater freedom in its place. And if ever the authority has to be imposed something of its essence is already lost.

Freedom and authority are not two disparate, mutually exclusive entities. Neither, in this life, can exist in isolation. Freedom is freedom only by the yardstick of authority and authority fulfils its true function only when it serves to increase freedom. The Bible is much more a book about liberty than it is a book about law and yet it is also a book of laws. Church history may be seen as a series of lurches from the libertarianism of the Bible as each man's sole guide to the authoritarianism of the laws derived from the Bible and codified in a Church. The Church of England has tried to be broad enough to contain both poles of those lurches.

Such a marriage between authority and freedom sounds attractive. But it is harder to attain than it might appear. To quote the Bishop of Chester, Dr Gerald Ellison: 'To be an Anglican requires many qualities which even some men of the highest religious genius have lacked. It requires courage to apply the individual conscience to the challenge of the Faith; it needs patience to wait until the answer to some problem not yet obvious is revealed, and the honesty to say on occasions, "I don't know". It needs the love to be tolerant with those whom we think misguided or foolish in their expression of their opinions. It needs the self-discipline to accept the demands of our Faith, not because we are told we must do so but because we believe such things to be true. Here is the true genius of Anglicanism and it is very precious.'[1]

What is true about individual freedom is equally true about the Communion as a whole. The Anglican Communion is insistent that there is no such thing as the Anglican *Church*. Rather there is a family of Churches and each is autonomous. Like grown-up members of a family, each finds pleasure in the family associations and each has the duty of considering the others when reaching a decision. But each has to live its own life in its own situation. One of the classic statements about the nature of the Anglican Communion is in the Encyclical Letter of the 1930 Lambeth Conference: 'This Communion is a commonwealth of Churches without a central constitution: it is a federation without a federal govern-

---

[1] *The Anglican Communion*, Seabury Press, Connecticut, U.S.A., 1960.

ment. It has come into existence, without any deliberate policy, by the extension of the Churches of Great Britain and Ireland beyond the limits of these islands.'

The 1968 Lambeth Conference (as had the 1948 and 1958 occasions) showed how these words have become a fundamental tenet of Anglican thinking: 'We are a family,' says the Report,[1] 'of autonomous Churches, varied and flexible, linked by ties of history, tradition, and living fellowship with the see of Canterbury, the focal point of our communion.

'In the face of God's majesty and love we often feel called to pursue a middle way, not as a compromise but as a positive grasp of many-sided truth. We have come to value reason and tolerance and to be comprehensive even at the expense of strict logic. We are prepared to live, both in fellowship and tension, with those who in some points differ from us.'

The 1930 Lambeth Conference Encyclical well describes what lies at the heart of the matter: 'Every Church of our Communion is endeavouring to do for the country where it exists the service which the Church of England has done for England–to represent the Christian religion and the Catholic Faith in a manner congenial to the people of the land, and to give scope to their genius in the development of Christian life and worship.' That vision has good biblical precedent. John, for example, wrote to 'the seven Churches of Asia' and he was no doubt aware that the Christians of Ephesus did not have to be identical with the Christians of Rome or Jerusalem. Certainly the context of their Christian life and the problems they encountered would be different.

In the twentieth century, with its inevitable logic of one world where all men must live as one family there is a vital truth here and its significance is secular as well as sacred. There are those who speak as if one world entails all humanity gradually becoming one great blur. There would be real loss if this happened. For just as some men have some gifts and other men have others, so with nations. Chinese are not identical with Indians and Welshmen are not identical with Eskimos. Each group of humanity has its own

[1] p. 141.

characteristics and the human race will prosper best not when each is submerged in some chimerical common man but when each puts his own distinctive gifts into the common pool. Anglicanism has recognised this. And it has also found that this counsel of perfection has its own built-in problems. Not least is the chaotic appearance such growth must have. Especially since this growth must involve trial and error and there must be mistakes as well as achievements. But the goal is worth pursuing. In fact, the goal *must* be pursued, for ultimately there is no other. Anglicans would never claim to have found the answer. But they believe they are facing in the right direction.

The Anglican Communion, like the Church of England, has accepted freedom as one of the prime virtues and accepted it as a positive philosophy, not as a casual *laisser-faire*. Yet in doing so, it has accepted a continuing problem – which sometimes becomes an agony. And conditions of the modern world are likely to make it more so. Once upon a time the details of the way an Anglican Church lived at the other end of the world might have been of little immediate importance to Englishmen. Now world communications mean that people come and go across the world and even when they do not move, the rest of the world is brought by television and other forms of immediacy into their own homes. Thus, to take but one example, an earthquake or some other disaster in a place like Japan is a personal experience of people living in London. They naturally ask what is their Church doing about helping people in Japan and especially their fellow-Anglicans among them. But the simple fact is that their Church can do little unless it has an international organisation.

The Anglican Communion increasingly finds that it needs some form of joint action in face of the unexpected. Alongside that stand the problems raised by growing relationships at two levels. The first is the growing relationship between Anglican Churches across the world, again one of the fruits of international communications. For relationships become more desirable as they become more possible. The other, and in many ways the more pressing, arises from the growing relationships between Anglicans and their fellow

Christians. Obviously local circumstances mean that these increase both at different rates and in different directions in various parts of the world. In one place the growth may be predominantly in connection with Roman Catholics, in another it might be with Protestants. In England, relations with Lutherans, who are few in number, can be a purely academic matter. In America, where they are many, it can be of great importance.

Again, the social conditions in which Anglican Churches have to work differ widely. In one country divorce may be relatively easy compared with another. The Church may be moved to vary its marriage laws in response to a given situation. But variation in one place must affect thinking in another. It is obviously desirable to have some common pool of information and that calls for organisation.

The Lambeth Conferences themselves might be seen as the beginning of such common action and organisation a hundred years ago but to do so would be to confer upon Anglicanism a discipline and a tidiness it has never had. Those Conferences set up their Lambeth Consultative Body before the turn of the century but that, too, was ineffective. It was not until the 1958 Lambeth Conference that any real action was taken. The result of this was the appointment of Bishop Stephen Bayne as Anglican Executive Officer, a post which depended very much more upon charisma than upon terms of reference and clearly delineated duties. He was followed five years later by Bishop Ralph Dean who still had no very obvious brief. Both men did superb work but it is characteristically Anglican that there is no way of assessing it statistically or otherwise. But the result was to convince the 1968 Lambeth Conference that it had to go further and accordingly it set up an Anglican Consultative Council with the Archbishop of Canterbury as President and with a full-time Secretary General and staff. It is to meet every two years while its Standing Committee is to meet annually. It has a bishop, priest or deacon and a lay person as its members from five Anglican Churches and a bishop plus a priest, deacon or lay person from the remaining eleven Anglican Churches and four other districts.

It is worth quoting in full its functions as stated in the Lambeth Conference Report:[1]

1. To share information about developments in one or more provinces with the other parts of the communion and to serve as needed as an instrument of common action.

2. To advise on inter-Anglican, provincial, and diocesan relationships, including the division of provinces, the formation of new provinces and of regional councils, and the problems of extra-provincial dioceses.

3. To develop, as far as possible, agreed Anglican policies in the world mission of the Church and to encourage national and regional Churches to engage together in developing and implementing such policies by sharing their resources of manpower, money, and experience to the best advantage of all.

4. To keep before national and regional Churches the importance of the fullest possible Anglican collaboration with other Christian Churches.

5. To encourage and guide Anglican participation in the Ecumenical Movement and the ecumenical organisations; to co-operate with the World Council of Churches and the world confessional bodies on behalf of the Anglican Communion; and to make arrangements for the conduct of pan-Anglican conversations with the Roman Catholic Church, the Orthodox Churches, and other Churches.

6. To advise on matters arising out of national or regional church union negotiations or conversations and on subsequent relations with united Churches.

7. To advise on problems of inter-Anglican communication and to help in the dissemination of Anglican and ecumenical information.

8. To keep in review the needs that may arise for further study and, where necessary, to promote inquiry and research.

It should be noted that this is the Consultative Council as agreed at the Lambeth Conference. At the time of writing it still needs the confirmation of some of the individual Churches.

It is probably true to say that such confirmation will be given. At the same time it is no less true to say that much of the giving will be grudging. Anglicans look at the Vatican or at a body like the

[1] p. 46.

Lutheran World Federation and many of them conclude that they do not want any central authority. The Lambeth Conference goes to great lengths to insist that the Council does not have authority in that sense. But Anglicans are by nature deeply suspicious of any central organisation. For they know the power of an institution to acquire its own vested authority. Bureaucracy does not appeal to the Englishman, and especially when in relation to his Church. In the next chapter we shall have to look at organisation within the Church of England and we shall find the same thing there.

Solvitur ambulando is much more the Anglican mind. Perhaps it was summed up by a prominent Anglican working in a Church organisation who insisted that his most urgent prayer was: 'Oh God, don't let the machine get me.' There is a Luddite streak in Anglicans when confronted by mechanisms of authority.

4

Establishment

We have tried to look into the mind of the Church of England and also into its soul. We have, all too cursorily, looked at how the Church of England came to be. The next thing is to look at its relationships and that, in the minds of most people, means first of all its relations with the State. Perhaps there is no more fertile a source of misunderstandings. The idea of a group of clergy paid by the Prime Minister and waiting for the post to bring next Sunday's sermon dictated from Downing Street is as widespread as it is fallacious. During the last war, the Ministry of Information actually did try suggesting sermon notes to clergy and very soon dropped the idea. And apart from hospital, prison forces' and embassy chaplains who are in the direct employ of the State, no clergy are paid by the State. Neither does the Church as an institution receive any money from the State.

Perhaps we ought first to spell out the 'right and privilege of Establishment'. To quote *Church and State, the Report of a Commission appointed by the Church Assembly, 1952*:[1] 'The particular characteristics of the Church of England are what constitutes the relationship which goes by the name of "establishment". These particular characteristics embrace both "rights and privileges' and on the other hand "restrictions and limitations", and it is not always easy to distinguish between them. The status of "establishment" includes the restriction to Anglican clergymen of the office of chaplain to the Speaker of the House of Commons and certain professorships and chaplaincies in the Universities of Oxford, Cambridge and Durham; the right of the Archbishop of Canterbury to crown the Sovereign; precedence in all religious services associated with events of importance in the national life; the repre-

[1] Church Information Office.

sentation of the Episcopate in the House of Lords; the requirement that the sovereign must join in communion with the Church of England; the right of the parish priest to celebrate marriages recognised as lawful, and his position as "persona" of his parish and not merely as minister of a gathered congregation.'

Those are the privileges. There are, argue some people, several advantages in addition. Those who favour Establishment point out that a Prime Minister is not likely to have inclinations towards any particular party within the Church of England and this has prevented each successive school of thought of this Church excluding the others. Furthermore, they argue, the Prime Minister is likely to make appointments which are more ecclesiastically adventurous, thus avoiding the colourless middle man who is so often the choice of a democratic electoral system. Again, a Prime Minister is likely to be accustomed to facing hard practicalities while theologians are more likely to be preoccupied with not immediately attainable ideals. It is good, so it is averred, that a bishop should be chosen for his ability to tackle realities rather than have someone who is 'sincere but. . . .'

Alongside these arguments must be listed other beneficial qualities of establishment. These include advantages for those who have done little to support the Church, for they have the effect of making the Church available when it is wanted. Because the clergy of the Church of England are charged to minister to all the people of their parishes, each person has the right to call on his parson – and there is a parson who is obliged to answer whether the call comes from dreary slum or remote hamlet. Every parishioner has a right to a seat in his parish church and to have his child christened there and, as long as there are no legal problems, to be married or buried there. This, of course, raises the charge that the Church of England appears to be satisfied with a very nominal form of religion. That is true. But any experienced parish priest will have many memories of how something which appeared nominal went very much deeper or how the merely superficial became entirely sincere when confronted with one of life's turning points.

Perhaps we have said enough for the moment to indicate that

the balance of advantage and disadvantage in regard to establishment is a fine one and facile judgements are ruled right out. But do Church leaders desperately cling to establishment as some ultimate vantage point? There are people who imagine that Disestablishment is the final bogey word which causes Anglican clergy rapidly to come to heel when it threatens them. Two archbishops seven and a half centuries apart explode such a delusion. The first clause of the Magna Carta declares that 'the Church of England shall be free', free, that is, to appoint its bishops and other leaders according to Canon Law. A prime promoter of that Charter was Stephen Langton, Archbishop of Canterbury. Ironically, Stephen Langton was suspended from office by the Pope for not supporting the king. But he certainly represented the mind of the English Church.

The second archbishop we cite is Dr Michael Ramsey, the hundredth Archbishop of Canterbury, who said in his Enthronement Sermon at Canterbury in 1961: 'Here in England the Church and the State are linked together, and we use that link in serving the community. But, in that service and in rendering to God the things that are God's we ask for a greater freedom in the ordering and in the urgent revising of our forms of worship. If the link of Church and State were broken, it would not be we who asked for this freedom who broke it, but those – if there be such – who denied that freedom to us.' Dr Ramsey has also frequently indicated that it is not only in respect of its forms of worship that the Church seeks freedom.

The general attitude of the Church of England can probably be described as not regarding establishment or disestablishment as sufficiently important to justify the expenditure of a great deal of time and emotion when there are more serious things to get on with. This chapter will have to spend more time on this topic. But perhaps we have established (and that word is deliberately used to indicate that it can have an innocence about it) that there are more important things to talk about even in the realm of Church and State relations. The Church must always be primarily concerned with getting on with its work. It is only when the State relationship interferes with that work in some essential manner that it becomes vital to make changes.

What is the Church's function towards the State? Perhaps it is necessary to remind ourselves first of the function of the State: it is to create the best conditions of life for its people. The State exists for man, not, as the totalitarians suggest, for its own sake. But anything which exists for man is an instrument of God whose will is man's plenitude. The State, then, no less than the Church, is under God and the whole tenour of the Bible says so. God is not a captive ecclesiastic working only on sacred ground but the only Lord of all history. Both Church and State are under God. This does not equate them. A husband and wife are both under the same vows to God but that does not make them identical. Indeed, it is vital that their diversity of function remains unimpaired. The Christian acknowledges that the State must retain its own integrity and he condemns the 'secular' State, divorced from religion, only when 'secular' means a total disregard for religion. Thus India and the United States are both countries which have separation between Church and State written into their constitutions but neither evinces any greater indifference to spiritual things than any other country.

We have, then, two entities: Church and State. If their functions were identical, then one of them would be superfluous. Yet both function under God. And each has a duty toward the other. What is the duty of the Church towards the State? If one may use a word which has become almost eviscerated, the simple answer is, love it.

Love it. Unhappily, the very use of that word can obscure a whole argument, for few words have felt more fatally the attrition of meaning which is the fate of words. Love is not a mawkish sentimentality. Love is not even an idealistic altruism. Love is the nature of God himself and its heart is creativity. When a man is in love, whether it be with a thing, like his work or his country, or with a person, like his wife, his whole being longs for the completeness of the object of his love. A man does not marry a girl in order to change her into something quite different but in order that he might devote his life to enabling her to become more than ever that with which he fell in love. The essential object of love is the fulfilment of the selfhood of the beloved.

The Church must love the State. It must, that is, desire the State to attain its own particular fulness. Immediately it becomes obvious that this loving can be neither mawkish nor weak. For mawkishness obscures the vision while the weak will never have the capacity to help toward fulness. One of the first things, then, that the Church must be able to do in relation to the State is to exercise the faculty of judgement. It must be able to assess the realities of the situation and it must have a standard by which those realities are measured. In passing, it is worth noticing that the Church, or something like it, with its objective standards and its external-to-the State viewpoint, is the only sort of organisation which can save the State from becoming so absorbed in its own aims and so content that anything which serves those aims must be right that it falls victim to an insidious totalitarianism.

The Church, then, must be able to exercise impartial judgement about the State. It is significant that in an England which has had establishment for so long, people should still regularly say about some evil 'Why doesn't the Church do something about it?' If one further analyses such a remark it is usually found to mean: 'Why don't the bishops *say* something about it?'

The idea that English people have cherished for centuries that the State is in some way over the Church has not deprived them of the memory that a function of the Old Testament prophets and all their successors has been to condemn whatever may be wrong in society around them and in the State which is its leader. Such an idea does not spring merely from history. It has its root right in the nature of man. For man is not an uneasy combination of mind, body and spirit but a single integrity. It is nonsense to say that the Church must care for man's spiritual condition and the State for his mental and physical condition, for man is not sometimes a disembodied spirit and sometimes a questing mind and sometimes a full-blooded body. He is always and ineluctably all three together. But if this is the case, not only does the Church have a responsibility for man's body and mind as well as his soul but also the State has a responsibility for his soul as well as his body and mind. Church and State can fulfil their functions only when they are partners, however that partnership may be defined by law or by custom. Therefore, it is not the function of the Church to speak out only at times of some major national evil but rather to be in continual conversation with the State–and conversation is a two-way process involving listening as well as speaking. It is the job of the State to be looking for the best ways of serving its citizens. It is the job of the Church constantly to be assuring the State that it is not doing this in some earthbound vacuum concerned with humans only as statistical units, but in the context of the fulness of man in the fulness of God. This does not prevent 'politics being the art of the possible' but it does imply constantly indicating that the possible has a wider horizon and richer demands than one might have thought. It does not prevent the State dealing with man as he is but it does insist that man as he is can only be assessed in the light of what it is man's capacity to become. The politician whose nose is tied to the often-depressing grindstone of human follies and failures can be lifted up by the Church's insistence on hope.

The Church's function is to love the State. The very words remind us that the State is not merely the bureaucracy it can only too easily become, especially in the complexities of modern life. Always there has been, increasingly there is, a tendency for the State to become a machine where all human relations between government and governed become dehumanised by a computer and forms filled in triplicate. It is impossible to love a machine. And this serves as a reminder that the State is not a collective of humanity but a group of men and women who remain individuals. Is it not only too easy nowadays for a man to get lost in a production line and to pass into nothingness with the poignant cry, 'I do not know what I am or who I am'? The Church which believes that God himself became man and thus forever honoured each individual man must have the continuing duty of watching for tendencies in the State which diminish a man. The Church must ever point out that if a State system of education is likely to produce

75

uniform robots or if a medical service reduces sick persons to 'cases' or if an industrial system treats honest craftsmen as mere 'hands in a factory', then it is under judgement and sentence must be passed. In this respect, the numbers who attend church regularly are totally irrelevant. The Apostles did not water down their statements about the ancient world because they were only eleven in number. Nor did their numerical insignificance rob their statements of power. Running right through the Bible is the concept of the 'remnant' and it is as relevant today as ever.

One of the interesting features of this remnant, whether we see it in the Jews mourning by the waters of Babylon or in a handful of people at the foot of the Cross, is its apparent insignificance by human standards. The remnant always illustrates that man's weakness is in a real sense God's opportunity. When men are strong, when a movement is vigorous and popular, there is always the impression that mountains can be removed without help from any external source. It is essentially through man's awareness of his limitations that God works. This is a lesson the Church knows intellectually and knows, too, as a matter of faith. But it rarely wants to put this bit of knowledge into practice. The Church is constantly tempted to seek power—always, of course, assuring itself that it will use that power when gained for the very best ends. It is as insidious and as lethal a temptation as can afflict the Church. And especially in the circumstances of the modern State. Government today, even in democracies, has open to it means of power which have no precedent. And power is always hungry for more power. There is a sense in which the more dedicated a politician is, the more dangerous he becomes, for he is apt to persuade himself that any means are justified if they secure the ends in which he believes. The occupational hazard of the modern State is a lust for organising society into the pattern it approves. It has no power of itself to save itself. Unless it has a standard outside itself it has no means whereby to judge itself. Since all states are open to this corruption, looking at other countries gives little help. The British, like many other peoples, have always prided themselves that the Law is a body which stands outside the State to judge the doings of the State. But today laws have become to a frightening degree a matter of administrative decree. And they have acquired the power to spawn further laws until the citizen gets lost in a codebook of prohibitions of which he may never have heard – how many motorists know how many laws they may break every time they drive a car?

All this power with all its manifestations gets concentrated in bureaucracy and the ordinary man seems helpless in face of it. The Church has a duty here and it is a hard one: it is to insist that each man has his rights and that civil liberties are not the optional extra of Utopia but a prime necessity at all times. It is a hard duty not least because it cannot be adequately safeguarded by bishops talking in the House of Lords or by any other means granted by establishment. Rather it is to be the constant burden of every parson and every parishioner as he finds an old lady caught in the toils of some Ministry or an old-age pensioner lacking some entitlement because of the complexity of filling in the requisite form. It must inevitably mean that the Church lives in tension, the tension of constant watchfulness and also the tension of having to tell the State, in the person of one of its officials, that he is rendering to Caesar rights over a person which belong only to God. This function of safeguarding human rights is born not of any 'establishment' but of the essential inner nature of the Church.

All this is a process of developing a national conscience and this is something which must be a prime duty of the Church. It is not the Church's function to tell Parliament what laws to make in order to try to force people to be good. It is the Church's calling so to influence the nation that Parliament comes to codify good laws which are the expression of an already existing feeling.

To help thus to create a national conscience can be costly and unpopular. To take an example: the Church knows that the compassion of Christ demands that a rich nation like ours should make sacrifices for underprivileged peoples overseas. There is reason to believe that many members of the Government are equally aware of that fact. Yet they dare not implement it until the nation as a whole is ready because such implementation involves an increase in national taxes. And Governments are very sensitive about getting public opinion on their side before taking such a step whenever it is possible. Bishops in the House of Lords may plead for legislation, cardinals and moderators may support them. But until each bit of the Church in each bit of the country is building up a body of conviction nothing significant is likely to happen.

The ramifications of this duty of the Church to create a national conscience are immense. They extend through the Board Rooms of big business and through the Council Chambers of Trade Unions, they must make their impact on the primers of the infants schools and on the leading articles written in Fleet Street, they must infiltrate the crowded arenas and must be felt in the loneliness of a bed-sitter. And they must constantly proclaim that the peace of God not only passes human understanding but also has the power to pass through any human barrier. It is a message so urgently needed by a generation living on the edge of panic.

All the time it has to be remembered that it is the people who are in the Board Rooms and Council Chambers, in the crowded arenas and in the lonely bed-sitters who, humanly speaking, make up the Church. This means that the Church in a very real sense must be not only sensitive to but also subject to the panic. It must feel the pains of life, even as its Lord did on the Cross. It must always be involved in the human situation and nothing except sin must be alien to it. At the same time, the Church must also be *outside* society and able to take an objective view of it. The Church must live in two worlds and yet not become schizophrenic, and each world must be equally real. For ultimately its whole task can be stated in one phrase: to bring the kingdoms of this world into being the kingdom of Our Lord and of his Christ, as the Seer of Patmos described it.

'Thy kingdom come . . .' As Christians say those words they know that the only raw material of the coming kingdom is the world as it is at this moment. There is then, a deep theological heart in the relationship between Church and State. But that does not mean that it can be spelled out in a simple formula.

The Bible does not give a lot of help about the nature of that relationship. Christianity started as a tiny Jewish sect on the remote fringe of an empire and there was little reason for its adherents to imagine that they would ever be in a position to want to formulate Church-State relations. The Christian Lord had accepted Caesar's authority about taxes and, with far more costly results, he had accepted Pilate's authority to sit in judgement over him. Paul commanded whole-hearted obedience to the civil authority and he himself appealed to it and got to Rome as a result. Perhaps most surprising, Peter could give a long exhortation on the respect due to the State including 'Honour the king' and that when the king was Nero, paradigm of evil and hater of Christians.

The early Church encouraged its members to keep State laws. At the same time, it went beyond them in laying upon those members things like marriage laws stricter than civil requirements and rules about the eating of meat and matters of Church discipline which had no parallel in the State system. Right from the beginning the Church has felt that it must call its own members to a higher form of living than it could demand of the outsider and accordingly it has to legislate for its own members while accepting the realities of a lower standard practised by those among whom they lived.

Christianity was a religion not sanctioned by law and therefore the very existence of the Church laid it open to attack. As long as it could be regarded as a Jewish sect it was fairly safe, for the Jews had a special dispensation for worship in the Roman empire. But the moment it began to spread around the ancient world, the situation became different. Christians were no longer Jews and therefore they were called upon to engage in idolatry, and more especially, emperor worship. Christians were not able to obey such a command. But neither were they able to persuade the civil authority that their disobedience sprang not from a disloyalty to the emperor but from a loyalty to God. Christians accordingly appeared unpatriotic. Persecution was the consequence which was entirely logical from the State point of view. Christians seemed able to accept this logic and even when the Bible does denounce the imperial machine as persecutor (Revelation 13 and 17) and where the cult of the emperor is denounced as anti-Christian (Revelation 2.13) the condemnation is not of the empire as such but of the empire as persecutor.

Then comes the great watershed of Church history, the alliance which began with Constantine, and Christians have been arguing ever since whether it was for good or for evil. Constantine recognised that the State had failed to suppress the Church. Whether from conviction that the Church held the truth or from expediency, he offered the friendly approach. The 'Edict of Milan' in 313 (which was not an edict nor did it issue from Milan) announced that all religions would be equally tolerated. There was to be no more persecution. Even more importantly in terms of consequences, the Church was recognised as a legal personality, able to accept gifts and own property. Clergy were given legal recognition equal to that of pagan priests. Constantine did not 'establish' the Church but the process had begun. Under his successor edicts were issued against heathenism as heathenism. Thus, by then, the State had declared for Christianity and before the fourth century had ended, heresy and paganism had become offences against the civil law. In effect, the discipline of Christians had nominally become the law of the State. And the State presented the bill. If the secular arm was used to suppress heretics then it could expect the religious officers to help in State duties. The value of bishops, amongst the best educated men of the day, as civil servants became obvious. But if a bishop was to be an important government official then the State obviously had some say in choosing who should be bishops. Then again, if the State was going to enforce Church laws, its voice had to be heard when those laws were being made. The Emperor, personification of the State, became a vital figure. No doubt none of this happened by a deliberate, or even perhaps by a conscious, process. In any case, Christians would have few worries about it for the Emperor was now a Christian and was 'the Lord's anointed'. 'You are bishops of matters within the Church; I also am the bishop ordained by God of matters without the Church,' said Constantine.

Gradually the distinction between Church and State became

blurred and the concept of a Christian Commonwealth, now operating as State, now operating as Church, grew up. And the idea of the ancient Israel as Church and State came back into men's minds. In a fully realised Christian commonwealth, maybe there would be no need to make a distinction between the methods of the State and the methods of the Church. But in more earthy situations such distinction is vital. The State has not only the right but also the duty to compel its citizens to accept its laws and to make those laws universally binding on all citizens. The Church has no such right. But it failed to recognise the fact. Gradually it came to be accepted that it was right to use force to bring men into the Church, to use force to keep them there once they had arrived, to use force to make them obedient to every ecclesiastical commandment. The Church fell victim to the illusion that it could persecute men into salvation. It was a corruption at the heart of the Church and it was also a distortion in its body, for it resulted in a theoretical membership far in excess of actual believers.

Then again, this confusion between Church law and State law meant that the Church's duty to teach absolute righteousness had to be watered down to match what the State could demand. Christian morality became equated with political expediency—and one of the results was the development of at least a notional double standard. Full Christian living was to be expected of the clergy and the religious orders but the word laity could be synonymous with laxity. The very idea of the Church as the total body of the faithful with one obedience differently expressed was wrecked.

There was also another explosive strand built into this concept. It was the idea that in any one form of society only one form of religion could be tolerated. The sordid features of the Reformation when all parties equally persecuted all parties found their birth here. Puritans, no less than Catholics, insisted that Church and State must be co-extensive. None of them wished to separate from the Church. But each insisted on moulding both Church and State to his own concept.

By medieval times the idea of the two-headed State, with Emperor and Pope in theory exercising equal imperium but in fact see-sawing for power, had reached its high-water mark. Even in England, always ready to be insular and suspicious of what happened on the continent, this duality was recognised. In Saxon times there were no separate Church courts and no clear distinction between national and ecclesiastical assemblies. Every Englishman was *de facto* member both of the State and of the Church so there was no point in making distinctions. There was never any dispute between Church and State. What did happen from time to time were disputes within the single body as civil and ecclesiastical officials jockeyed for power. But underlying all this in England was a further unease which did not affect the continent. For the supreme ecclesiastical authority was a foreigner living in Italy and he was not above making arrangements with foreign princes whose interests might be hostile to those of England. If these interests seemed likely to injure either the bodies or the property of Englishmen then the secular arm waved the more strongly. The Royal supremacy meant that civil officials must have the right to decide what questions ecclesiastical officials were allowed to refer to their papal lord. It was not that the king was claiming any spiritual authority. He was just making sure that no one diminished his civil authority. He was, so to speak, supervising the Church from the outside.

But the king was also, *de facto*, the leading layman of the Church and as such it was his duty to be her defender. The Church in England could not adequately do her work if ideas more suited to the Mediterranean were given too much force. Or if the Roman authority seemed to err in favour of princes who lived nearer him. The papal statement that only spiritual authority was claimed was not always sustained by events, especially when a weak king found that concessions to Rome could strengthen his domestic position. The fourteenth century had found it necessary to have its statutes of *Praemunire* to limit papal sway. England was already showing itself tired of papal exactions. So, in 1534, Convocation declared that 'The Pope of Rome hath no greater jurisdiction conferred upon him by God in Holy Scripture, in this kingdom of England, than any other foreign bishop.' Three years earlier, Henry had claimed to be 'Supreme Head of the English Church and Clergy' and Convocation accepted the title with the vital clause added 'so far as the law of Christ allows'. In a letter addressed to the Convocation of York Henry plainly disclaimed any new authority in spiritual matters. In 1534 Parliament recognised him as the 'only supreme head on earth of the Church of England'. And the title 'supreme head' seemed to worry nobody. Cranmer could write, 'Every king in his own realm is supreme head. . . . Nero was head of the Church, that is in worldly respect of the temporal bodies of men, of whom the Church consisteth: for so he beheaded Peter and the Apostles. And the Turk, too, is head of the Church of Turkey. . . . The king is head and governor of his people which are the visible Church . . . wherein he was named supreme head of the Church, there never was any other thing meant.'

Given such a definition, the Church would have little reason to worry. But Henry was a strong king. And he was not willing to let his supremacy be a matter of name only. Accordingly he showed how he interpreted his right to exercise 'full power and authority . . . to visit, repress, reform . . .' and the consequences were savage. Monasteries, for example, were dissolved and their goods appropriated. There can be no doubt that many of them needed reform. But that does not mean liquidation. The Church became powerless in Henry's hands. The essential point, however, is that it did not stop being the Church, with all its ancient order intact.

The title 'supreme head' was continued by Edward VI and even by Mary up to the time of her marriage in 1554. It was then dropped and has never since been revived. Elizabeth claimed only to be 'Supreme Governor', insisting that the honour of being head of the Church of England 'is due to Christ alone, and cannot belong to any human being soever'. She went further than that and insisted that the mind of the Church must be sought before the monarch or Parliament may legislate for it. In 1572 she forbade Parliament to discuss bills concerning religion 'unless the same should first be considered and be liked by the clergy', and in 1593 she followed that up with a note to the Speaker, 'If you perceive any idle heads . . . which will meddle with reforming the Church or transforming the commonwealth and do exhibit any bills to such purpose, that you receive them not, until they be viewed and considered of those who it is fitter should consider of such things and can better judge of them.'

Perhaps we can now list some of the consequences of all this.

1. No Englishman can claim to be outside the jurisdiction of the Crown in virtue of any office he may hold in the Church. The Archbishop of Canterbury is subject to the same laws as the rest of us and none will grumble at that.

2. The monarch is to be the guardian of all forms of justice. When in the civil courts judges act in his name they do not make the laws: they only interpret and administer them. Similarly when the monarch exercises authority as Supreme Governor he does not make the Church's laws nor can he alter them but he is responsible for seeing that the Church's own laws are properly observed.

3. It is the monarch's duty to see that the relationship between Church and State is kept in balance and each side faithfully adheres to its own part of the relationship.

All this is surely quite unexceptionable. But we have not finished.

4. The authority which the Crown gained was originally conferred upon the monarch as a person and as a loyal son of the Church. Constitutional changes have meant that real power has passed from the monarch to the Prime Minister and the Cabinet. In recent times that power has appeared to be increasingly concentrated in a few hands, with ministerial decrees taking much of the place once held by parliamentary acts. This transformation of a personal monarch into a heterogeneous group, for which religious belief of any sort is not a condition of membership, has exposed the Church to real dangers. There is, in principle, no reason why every member of the House of Commons, and hence the Prime Minister and the Cabinet, should not be a non-Christian. There is also no reason, in principle, why the authority of Parliament should not be used to create a bench of bishops (and many other Crown appointments including university professorships) which was amenable to whatever philosophy the Government wished to

promulgate. It is perfectly true that the Prime Minister can only appoint to an office. He cannot confer spiritual authority. That can only come through consecration at the hands of the Church. But the system remains indefensible – apart from the peculiarly English argument that it works. It does indeed work, many would say, better than some of the electoral systems which operate in other parts of the Anglican communion. But the dangers are obvious.

5. Another grievance is that because of this system the Church cannot legislate for itself even in regard to its own inner life of worship. Before anything can become part of the law of the Church it has to gain the approval of the Crown and of Parliament as well as the Convocations. When Parliament was, in the old days, really a House of Anglican laymen, this may have had much to justify it. But it was scarcely edifying to see Scottish and Irish, as well as English, non-Christians pontificating on a matter like the disestablishment of the Church in Wales a generation ago. And since no one would want to see the reintroduction of religious tests before a man can become an M.P. and therefore one cannot expect any major change in the nature of the House of Commons, then the question of freeing the Church from its domination becomes a real one.

The first step towards such freedom for the Church of England occurred in 1919 when Parliament passed the Enabling Act which set up the National Assembly of the Church of England – known more familiarly as the Church Assembly or irreverently as the 'Church Ass' 'to deliberate on all matters concerning the Church of England and to make provision in respect thereof'. For a significant half-century this Assembly was the Church of England's 'Parliament', so even though it is now being superseded by synodical government it demands its place in this book.

The Church Assembly was charged with the duty of initiating Church legislation in such a way that it had a reasonable chance of getting the approval of Parliament. The Church Assembly consisted[1] of a House of Bishops, which included all the members of

---

[1] Changes taking place at the time of writing made it difficult to decide the appropriate tense of verbs in this section.

the two Upper Houses of Convocation, a House of Clergy, consisting of all the members of the two Lower Houses of Convocation and a House of Laity, elected every five years by the representative electors of the Diocesan Conference. The Assembly was debarred from issuing pronouncements on matters of theology. These were reserved for the Convocations though it had become customary for Convocations to seek the opinion of the House of Laity on important theological matters.

Although it is something of a diversion, it is best at this point to say a word about Convocations. These are the ancient assemblies of the clergy of the Church of England and there is one for Canterbury and one for York. They date back to the seventh century. At first they included only bishops but in the thirteenth century representatives of the clergy, called Proctors, were added. In the early centuries it was through the Convocations that the clergy taxed themselves. The powers of Convocations were much limited by Henry VIII and one consequence is that the life of each Convocation terminates with the life of each Parliament and Proctors have to be re-elected. The Convocations were prorogued from 1717 to 1852. They meet for about four days two or three times a year. Both Convocations can, if they choose, meet together but they are entirely separate bodies and neither can speak for the Church of England.

To return to the Church Assembly. Its method of procedure seemed on the surface to be exceeding clumsy. First the Church Assembly had to decide that legislation on some point seemed desirable. This then became embodied in a 'measure' in which form it went on for discussion by a Legislative Committee of the Assembly. It next moved to a special Ecclesiastical Committee of both Houses of Parliament which then went over it in detail and drafted a report on the measure indicating whether it thought the measure good or bad, and more especially commenting on how it might affect any constitutional rights of any of the subjects of the realm. Before being presented to Parliament this report had to be returned for comment to the Legislative Committee of the Assembly at which point both committees could confer. The

Legislative Committee then had to decide whether to present the measure to Parliament or, if the omens were inauspicious, to withdraw it, the object being to avoid as far as possible any unhappy confrontation between Parliament and the Assembly. After the measure had been presented to Parliament, any member of either House could propose a resolution that it be submitted to the Crown for the Royal Assent. If this gained the approval of both Houses and subsequently received Royal Assent, the measure had all the force of any other Act of Parliament.

It is important to notice that while Parliament could accept or reject any measure, it had no power to alter it.

One good effect of the Enabling Act was that whereas the Church formerly had to plead for Parliamentary time which was grudgingly given before there could be any changes, even in minutiae, after the Act a considerable amount of Parliamentary time was saved thus making Members more amenable to Church matters.

6. Another consequence which disturbs many churchmen is that in cases of ecclesiastical offences the final court of appeal is the Judicial Committee of the Privy Council, which could be an entirely secular body consisting of non-Christians (though since 1876 two bishops have been added as assessors). In the Middle Ages the final appeal was to the Pope. When this ended at the Reformation there grew up a Court of Delegates the members of which were appointed by the Crown. In 1833, however, an Act of Parliament, carried without the consent of the Church and as a result of muddle rather than deliberate policy, transferred the final appeal to the Judicial Committee. The odd thing is that this Committee has no power to impose spiritual penalties for spiritual offences. It cannot, for example, excommunicate or deprive a man of Holy Orders. The result has been a court to which clergy are subject but which has little power to inspire their confidence. This has not been conducive to good order and harmony and much of the 'clerical lawlessness' of the Church of England can be attributed to this.

All of which makes a formidable list of unwelcome consequences of the present form of establishment of the Church of England. It would seem obvious that the Church ought to be making strenuous efforts to change this. That has not been the case. In the first place, as we have already said, the Church has always seemed to have more important things to get on with and regards the debate on establishment as not of high priority. In the second place, the list of objections look more impressive on paper than they turn out to be in actual practice. However much the jeremiads may lament 'post-Christian' England, the fact remains that we are still not living in an atheist State and therefore the Parliamentary connections do not prove to be as lethal as theory might suggest. In the fourth place, the Church has learned that in the one great modern example where Parliament has reversed the decision of the Church about its own affairs, that is, in regard to the revised Prayer Book, there are very many Churchmen who have come to the conclusion that Parliament was right (though perhaps accidentally) and actually did the Church a favour by making it think again. And, in the fifth place, when Churchmen come to consider the disabilities of the present form of establishment they do not find it easy to know whether they want disestablishment or another form of establishment.

For establishment in itself is not necessarily a crippling evil. The Church of Scotland, which is Presbyterian, is evidence of that. It is as much established in Scotland as the Church of England is in England. Yet it appoints its own officers, it has freedom to legislate for itself and such legislation is recognised as valid in the civil courts, it has a complete system of Church courts and it has spiritual autonomy. It was interesting to note that when, in 1969, the Queen visited the General Assembly (instead of appointing a Lord High Commissioner as usually happens) she did not open or close meetings but only 'observed the proceedings', thus acknowledging that this Church is at once established and free.

The problem of establishment does not lie in some malevolent connotations of the word. Rather it rests on the way in which the Church of England was established and the time at which it happened. Establishment does not mean creation. The State in

England has never in any way suggested that it founded the Church of England. What establishment means is that at a given moment, the process began by which the law of the land settled the government of the Church of England as it was at that moment. 'Henry VIII froze the Church of England' so someone said. And the moment at which that happened was one when the Church of England was in process of settling its *persona* and resuming its ancient nature after the break with Rome. It was a moment which caught the Church without its own machinery for self-administration. Every other Church in this country is subject to the civil law—the Free Churches can own land and safeguard their ownership by appeal to the civil courts, a Free Churchman dismissed from his post can contest that dismissal in the civil courts, an atheist who feels he has some grudge against, say, the Roman Catholic Church can resort to the processes of the law if he can persuade legal authorities that he has a case. There is a famous example. When in 1900 a minority of the Free Church of Scotland took their brethren to law because they were uniting with the United Presbyterian Church to form the United Free Church, the 'Wee Frees' won the challenge on doctrinal grounds. Consequently the minority acquired the property of the whole former Church. The decision was manifestly unfair—as was demonstrated by a subsequent Act of Parliament redressing the situation—but the law had to be operated as it stood, even within a Church. There is, perhaps, an even more striking example. The Board of Deputies of British Jews, founded in 1760, is an entirely Jewish organisation elected by synagogues and other Jewish bodies. It exists to look after all matters affecting the welfare of British Jews and especially to see that no Jew suffers disability by reason of his religion. It has received full statutory recognition from the Government and it is recognised as the official mouthpiece of the Jewish community. It is therefore, within its own limitations, part of the law of the land and can have full recourse to that law.

All religious bodies are subject to the law and have the full privileges of the law. But most of them have been allowed to set up their own bodies of doctrine and their own rules of procedure before the law comes to bear on them. The Church of England, growing alongside the growth of the kingdom of England, never had a moment when it could claim to have arrived and to have finally defined its faith and order. It never became externalised to the State and it has never therefore been able to define its being apart from the State. This raises an interesting question. If the Church of England were disestablished how could it draw up a doctrinal statement and a constitution which would satisfy all its members? Yet a non-established Church must have such or it cannot be a *persona* in the eyes of the law. Paradoxically the Church of England has a freedom deriving from establishment which it could lose without it. Canon Selwyn Gummer, born and brought up a Free Churchman, says 'The Church of England, I found, was safeguarded against the dangers of the Free Churches by *its very freedom*. O paradox. Here was unity in things essential, tolerance in things non-essential, and charity in all things. . . . I had learnt what an Anglican priest once claimed "The Church of England is the only Free Church in England".'[1]

But in theory and in many ways in practice, it remains bound by the State. Yet such is the English capacity for getting by. Even though the statements made above about the Church of England being tangled in the law are legally true, in practice they are becoming less and less true. The Church of England in recent years has moved a long way towards more overt benefits of freedom. It has done so with the full knowledge of the State. And the formula has been a paradoxical informality of permissive experiment and trial runs.

Thus the Book of Common Prayer as appended to the Act of Uniformity still remains the only strictly legal Prayer Book in the Church of England. It was accepted by the Convocations–i.e. the Church's own government–and then went to Parliament where it was passed as a schedule to the Act of Uniformity. Where Parliament has made an act, only Parliament can alter it. But you will find very few churches which adhere rigidly to its forms. The christening of a baby in the House of Commons chapel is not likely

[1] *They Became Anglicans*, ed. D. Morgan, Mowbray, 1959, p. 57.

to be in the form of service appended to the Act of Uniformity and thus the only one legally recognisable by the House of Commons.

We have moved a very long way from the early nineteenth century when the Church stood for little more than the State in its occasional spiritual mood. That nadir was already being influenced by the Evangelical Revival and its evils were soon to be underlined by the Oxford Movement with its insistence that the Church is the Body of Christ not the arm of the State. The validity of Establishment came more and more to be questioned. Alongside that came the growth of the independent Churches of the Anglican Communion across the world, sometimes in countries where British colonialism had made no impact and occasionally where even British culture was something alien. Such overseas Churches had little connection with the State and even the most Erastian of Establishment supporters came to realise that Anglicanism does not require any special understanding with the secular power. Its comprehensiveness does not depend on establishment. The existence of the Church in Wales as disestablished from 1920 drove this point home. As, through all its constitutional developments, the character of the English State has changed so the relationships of this Church with the State have changed. It has not come about by violent revolution, nor can one tie up the change in a historical or any other sort of formula. It has not led to rousing and lasting debates on Establishment and neither Church nor State has felt called upon to arouse public emotions towards a new relationship. But changes there have been. Today there is also an important new factor affecting the establishment of the Church of England. It is the move towards Christian unity. How can anyone expect, for example, Methodists not only to accept episcopacy but also accept that a Prime Minister by his sole judgement is the right person to appoint them? How can Free Churchmen with their long tradition of informal worship bind themselves to a Church whose worship is not only formal but is further restrained by a secular Parliament? On the other hand, there is no small amount of evidence that Free Churchmen would not welcome a root and branch disestablishment of the Church of England. What they, by and large, seem to desire is what every Anglican ought to long for—a Church-State relationship suited to twentieth-century pluralism rather than to the medieval synthesis.

But changes there already have been. And as these words are being written, we stand on the eve of further and perhaps major forward steps in the direction of Church freedom.

One move in this direction is the setting up of a General Synod of the Church of England. The half-century since the Enabling Act set up the Church Assembly has been a period of steady transition in the government of the Church of England. Many factors, and not least the increasing importance given to the thinking and status of the laity, are accelerating this change. The introduction of synodical government, which supersedes the provisions of the Enabling Act, aims at giving the laity a full share in church government at all levels. The General Synod, with its family of Diocesan Synods, Deanery Synods and Parochial Church Councils, can debate and legislate on any matter concerning the Church of England. It can also determine doctrine, a right hitherto reserved to the Convocations. It has thus assumed the spiritual and legislative authority of the Convocations and also the legislative powers of the Church Assembly. Like the housewife who holds on to things 'because they may come in handy', however, the Church of England has not disbanded the Convocations. They will continue to meet, perhaps inviting the House of Laity to join them from time to time. But it is not easy to see quite what their real function will be. When Canon (now Dean) E. W. Kemp moved the resolution by which the Convocation of Canterbury would transfer its powers to the General Synod he said it was 'in a sense the most momentous thing which had come before Convocations since the passing of the Submission of the Clergy Act' (by which, in 1532, Convocations surrendered to the demands made by Henry VIII). Quite certainly, synodical government was talked about for long enough before it was achieved. But whether or not it was that momentous, only time will tell.

What is fairly certain is that the average Anglican in his average pew is not likely to find this new form of government on its own stimulating him to some fiery new crusade. For the average Anglican is inclined to leave the government of his Church to someone else. He is, so to speak, not politically minded on Sundays. He is willing to do great deeds for his own local church but beyond that he rapidly loses interest. Easter vestries and other general parochial meetings are rarely well attended and complex ecclesiastical structures which seem so vital to those who labour over them in Westminster get little space on parish agendas or in the thoughts of congregations.

Perhaps their instinct is right. For any Church's organisation is inevitably a clutter of history struggling to adapt to the contemporary. For the Church of England, with its emphasis on comprehensiveness, it is hard to see how such machinery can fail to be cumbersome—and therefore remote. The ordinary Churchman keeps feeling that what the Church really needs is not complexity, nor even, ultimately, efficiency. Rather must its mark be a spontaneity of life bubbling from its deep inner resources. A degree of consistency and uniformity are essential. But they must never throttle the initiative of a Luther or a Wesley. At least the skeleton of structure there must be. But it is a hindrance when it is ossified and arthritic. For then the power of the Spirit must find other outlets. To provide a channel for that power is what Church structure is about. Let the builders never forget the Cornerstone. The Church must forever be listening to a voice which could be saying 'Destroy this temple and in three days I will build it up'.

5

The Clergy

Back in 1746 Lord Chesterfield told his son: 'Parsons are very like other men, and neither the better nor worse for wearing a black gown.' He was very much nearer the mark than the sentiment which Sydney Smith attributed to the French: 'There are three sexes—men, women and clergymen.'

Those two quotations came easily to mind and there are very many more which have also become part of the coinage of our language. The parson is probably a more frequent figure in English literature than any other character and he is surely more variously described. The spectrum from villainy to sanctity is his and to try to assess the fundamentals of his character we shall need a firm handrail. Paul Burrough provided one when, after a breadth of experience not given to every man, he became Bishop of Mashonaland, Rhodesia, at a critical moment in its history. He was asked how he conceived his work there. His reply was: 'to try to set myself free to the relentless logic of the love of God in this as in any other country in the world. To be a servant of the servants of God, but, at the same time, never to be scared of leadership.'

One point must be firmly and immediately made. What Paul Burrough was describing was not a calling exclusive to bishops nor even to clergy in general. All Christians have the vocation to be utterly exposed to the divine love so that they may acquire the character of servanthood which that love delineated in Christ and make that servanthood so real that it can emerge as leadership when the needs of those to be served demand it. Jesus's words, 'As the Father hath sent me, even so send I you' were universally addressed to all his followers even though their fulfilment was not to work out in some monochrome routine identical for every man. There are indeed 'diversities of operations' and to one is given the word of wisdom and to another the gifts of healing, and none of these gifts depend on whether the recipient is bond or free, male or female. All that, however, does not mean that male and female, bond and free, are identical.

In recent years there has been a steady rediscovery of the meaning of Peter's words: 'Ye are a chosen generation, a royal priesthood, an holy nation, a peculiar people', as addressed to all who have been baptised. This rediscovery, which many would claim as an insight given to the Church of England at the Reformation, has recently been visible in the Roman Catholic Church no less than in the Protestant and it is important and right. Nevertheless, there remains an identifiable body of men called 'The Clergy' and it deserves our attention. The trouble is that a reading of English literature together with the implications of remarks commonly made suggests that this body is identifiable for the wrong reasons. Time after time one comes across examples of people singling out the clergy either for some quality they are assumed to have in themselves or for some peculiar effect which is assumed to have rubbed off from their circumstances. Thus you find many who will imply by their behaviour that swearing is somehow more heinous in the presence of a parson. And perhaps the most ironic examples are the characters who run from the Epistle to Timothy's 'those who having a form of godliness creep into houses and take silly women captive' through Langland's wenching pardoner to Sinclair Lewis's pious but priapic evangelist. Literature seems to suggest that while parsons may be lechers their lechery is somehow different from other men's. Perhaps one of the functions served by the clergy is that the rest of society projects its own faults on to them and, like scapegoats of old, they, bearing the sins of the people on their heads, are driven out into some sort of mental wilderness.

'To try to set myself free to the relentless love of God' can indeed result in a man's accepting the burden of Christ who, outside the city walls, bore human sin on a cross. But no layman must be allowed to indulge himself in the fantasy that by paying someone to be a parson he can leave all spiritual things to the professional. You do not serve a man by castrating his own spiritual powers or making his spiritual effort otiose.

Many generally accepted ideas of what the clergy is for need re-examination both radical and ruthless. Fortunately–though, perhaps, painfully–the social changes of our day are forcing such a reappraisal upon lay and cleric alike. But before one can examine changes one must look at what is being changed. We shall start by thinking about the function of the average parson, for to the majority, he is the Church. Bishops are seen as mysterious figures who hide away in the House of Lords and deacons as tyros who change their status to priests as soon as they can. The English parson, with his myriad images in our cultural life, is the one we meet. It would be tempting to begin this study of the parson by following him down the highways and byways of history and literature. There we could trace all sorts of fascinating things–like the influence on English public life of the vicarage families with their astonishingly high proportions of nationally famous names. Or we could follow the various ingredients in this popular image from the fact of someone like George Herbert to the fiction of the wan curate hovering in the pages of *Punch*. But there is an urgency of consideration and a quantity of matter to consider in the contemporary world that do not allow time for backward glances. Except one which goes to the root.

Thirteen centuries ago, St Theodore, an Asiatic Greek, became Archbishop of Canterbury. He took his job seriously and one of his first actions was to visit the whole Church of England with a view to deciding how it could best be organised. One of the consequences was that the whole country was divided into parishes. Every corner fell into some parish boundary. Thus did the Church of England acknowledge that it had a duty to serve every individual in the land whether humble peasant in some remote cot or proud duke in his castle.

To each of these parishes was assigned a *persona*, a legal 'person' by whom the property of God in the parish was actually held. He was the identity of the parish. He was the responsible person, the one to sue or to be sued. Thus was born the concept of the parson as a 'personage'.

The connection between parson and parish is important; for it means that social changes in the parish must inevitably affect the nature of the parson, even if there were no theological reasons for such changes. In recent times our English public life has been almost totally transformed and accordingly the English parson has been subjected to a revolution more transforming than at any other period. Even the decree that there should be celibacy (not until the eleventh century) or the acceptance that there needn't (at the time of the Reformation) had less effect on the parson, either personally or professionally, than the social changes of today. Inevitably and rightly, therefore, people are asking what is the function of a parson in the light of these changes. No group of men ask this question more vociferously than parsons themselves. This is no example of an institution being attacked from the outside but rather it demonstrates the continually renewing capacity for self-examination which lies at the heart of the Church.

But before we go on to changes, we must clarify our picture of a parish. A parish is a geographical area with clearly defined boundaries. It is set in a rural deanery, an archdeaconry and a diocese, which is headed by the bishop. In the majority of cases a parish has one clergyman who is its incumbent and mostly he has one parish only, though plurality is allowed. In his parish an incumbent may have assistant curates and deaconesses to help him. The incumbent is appointed by a patron who has no further authority once the appointment is made and the Church has to see that he is suitably housed to allow him to do his job. Up to recently, a parish had to have at least one building set apart for worship and this was the parish church. In this church all parishioners not excluded by some specific reason have clearly defined rights in regard to baptism, marriage, burial and so on. Each parish has its own lay organisation of churchwardens, parochial church council and annual meeting.

One of the consequences of the parish set-up is that each unit has shown a tendency to become a little kingdom on its own with the power to build up emotional loyalties in the minds of parishioners who resist any sort of change. There are several factors now operating to break down such autonomy. The first is synodical government (see page 92) which comes into operation in 1970. The next is the consequences of the document *Partners in Ministry* (the 'Paul Report')[1] which, very briefly, suggests that instead of individual incumbents retaining their present autonomy the clergy of a diocese should be treated as a team and therefore it should be possible to move them to points of greatest need and to secure a greater uniformity of housing and stipends than has previously existed. This report will be debated in 1970. A third item is the Pastoral Measure which came into force in April 1969.

The heart of this Measure is the setting up of a Pastoral Committee for each diocese. This can make proposals to the bishop for the better ordering of pastoral care where circumstances call for it. Among its functions are to examine existing spheres of work and see if they fit present conditions, to see that conditions of service and payment of those engaged in pastoral work are as equitable as possible and to look at the needs of individual parishes in such matters as buildings—which will mean a very much greater flexibility of decision in regard to the closure of a church which no longer fulfils pastoral needs. Since the Measure has tried to keep in creative tension both the urgency of action in many places and the need to do all things in love and goodwill (thus involving complicated consultations and checks and balances) it has become fairly intricate. In any case, it is academic to judge a Measure by its written words until one has an opportunity of seeing how it works. Our primary point here is that it has considerably weakened the previously almost inviolate image of a parish and provided new opportunities for the Church to meet a situation as it exists rather than as it once was. Thus we are likely to see a considerable development of team ministries in place of the former one man per geographical unit arrangement. Whereas under the former way, authority had rested in the one man who was incumbent, in future it will be possible to have a 'college of clergy', all enjoying incumbent status, running a group of parishes with specialists among

[1] Church Information Office, 1967.

their number giving particular attention to things like youth work or industrial chaplaincies.

All this has an importance much greater than is immediately obvious. Previously, practically all clergy have assumed that after a few years as assistant curates they would spend the rest of their lives single-handed running a parish (in 1967 78 per cent of all incumbents in England held a solo ministry). The man who could do infinitely better work in a large slum parish as an assistant in charge of youth work was nevertheless made to feel that something was wrong if within relatively few years of his ordination he had not become incumbent of at least a tiny rural sphere, even though as a general practitioner he might be much less effective. Again, the one-man one-parish system has laid unwelcome sorts of responsibility upon many incumbents. Thus a man who was a gifted natural leader would find that all the real decisions of the parish soon devolved upon him and there would grow in his mind the fear of something approaching paternalism. For however much a man seeks the co-operation of the laity, there are types of parishes where local conditions do not produce many people with leadership qualities. On the other hand, an incumbent who, for reasons which perhaps had little to do with him, such as the proximity of several other churches in a relatively depopulated area, has an empty church could hardly help getting a bit depressed about his implied ineffectiveness because as long as he is on his own there is no one else to share the blame. The mobility of population in this country has contributed much to this and a Church which let its parish boundaries remain static in such a situation could hardly fulfil its pastoral duties. There is no room for the anomaly of one man in a new housing area responsible for 40,000 people and within a couple of miles of him another man in an ancient country parish responsible for 400.

Again, one of the fruits of English history and of English devotion is the rash of church buildings standing lonely among the offices in what were once thickly populated areas. Thus in the single square mile of the City of London with its total resident population of 4,500 there are 43 church buildings in regular use alongside a cathedral into which the whole resident population could get at one time. The ethics as well as the economics of maintaining all those churches in a world with millions starving are more than dubious. And the effect on an incumbent of striving to find the resources to heat and light the building and to repair the roof or whatever is disastrous. It is perfectly true that a church has many functions in addition to housing a congregation (Salisbury cathedral will hold a couple of thousand people but when it was built the total population of Salisbury was measured only in hundreds: that building is an act of worship in itself as well as a roof over worshippers' heads). But to use these arguments as reasons in themselves for expensive maintenance is to betray a wrong sense of values. And it is to lay upon the incumbent the temptation of regarding fund-raising or pew-filling as the final ends for which he was ordained.

The Pastoral Measure must inevitably alter the traditional idea of the parish church, there forever with its incumbent enjoying a freehold which is for all practical purposes a life-ownership. It is a major change in the government of the Church of England and its implementation will quite certainly lead to many grievances. The handful of old loyalists in a downtown church left remote as the tide of population has receded will not take easily to the closure of their beloved building. And the incumbent who feels any sense of insecurity will wonder about his future. Yet *ecclesia semper reformanda* and the changes in the human condition which the Church is now called to serve make it inevitable that this must be a moment of such reforming. It is to those changes that we must now turn, however briefly.

The first to be mentioned is what might be called 'the flight from institutionalism'. Every institution in our country – and throughout western Europe – is up before the bar of judgement. Politics and the forms of government, education and the shape of the university, economics and the management of the State, art and the traditional forms of its expression, God and his images and their incarnation in the Church, all are subjected to a rigorous re-examination. Superficially it would seem that the Church is failing to pass this examination and we have become accustomed to having the world point to empty pews. A little knowledge of history shows that there have been empty pews at many previous periods and they have refilled. Also that there have been full pews for the wrong reasons from time to time. What is surely significant today is the amazing amount of attention that is given to the concept of God and the way the continuing debate keeps breaking into the most unexpected places—like the interviewing of pop stars on Radio One. If God is dead, his obituaries are taking an unconscionable time. What is surely happening is that the mind of the twentieth-century, scientifically conditioned man, child of the open, pluralist, permissive society, is being exploded into a new and larger vision of God and the pews need some adjustment to take this. The religiousness of contemporary man can hardly be doubted. It is his religious habits which are changing. And if the Church cannot take account of this it must expect to be rejected. What is so encouraging is that the initiation of this debate about God and how to acknowledge him comes from within the Church itself. It was a *bishop* who wrote *Honest to God* and no one who knows him can doubt John Robinson's devotion and integrity. Alongside this goes the fact that public opinion polls as well as the constant private experience of the clergy make it obvious that we are a long way from any public anti-clericalism. The avidity with which the local community still seeks its parson to open the flower show or to join the coach tour is evidence that parsons are widely, perhaps as widely as ever, accepted, even though society may temporarily have lost sight of their true function.

It is the nature of those who do the accepting that we must examine. What is happening is that society can now do more efficiently much of what was once left to the parson. Take the mass media which are the greatest single influence on men today. It is little over a century since Northcliffe, father of the popular newspaper, was born. Radio and television are very much of this generation. They all speak incessantly and the parson has lost his oracular status as the only source of adult teaching. Today he must have the encyclopaedic coverage of a newspaper if he is to touch on all his parishioners' interests. And those who listen to the country's best speakers performing on the screen insist that their parson preaches like some electronic Chrysostom or take the consequences. At the same time, the schools which were once either run by the Church or not run at all have not only become universally available but have also become transformed into highly professional enterprises with well-trained staff and highly competent equipment. The Church welcomes those schools. When it began providing formal education it was its duty (though perhaps not its human inclination) to work itself out of a job.

Another area in which the Church has largely worked itself out of a job is in what we have come to call the welfare state with its at least notional guarantee of social security. No longer is the parson approached as the only available source of an admission ticket to the local hospital or the purveyor of coal and food to a needy widow, no longer does he have to fill in forms for an illiterate or make sure that the poor box has enough funds to provide a decent burial. Again, this is something the parson is glad about. He was never trained as a universal provider. He took on these duties because there was no one else to do them and he did them only at the expense of his time—and much of his personal money. His object was to fulfil the compassion of Christ. But no profession could have so large a chunk removed from its diary without a radical reappraisal of its function. Not, let it be noted, that the Church no longer has a place in our social services. Indeed, if it neglected an oversight of the bureaucracy which those services create they could soon degenerate. And no bureaucracy is ever going to cover comprehensively the idiosyncrasies of human need. The welfare state will always have gaps and it is only the voluntary agency which will fill them. There is also another factor in all this which reflects on the status of the clergy since it has the effect of reducing their numbers. Formerly if a man had a vocation to a life which was primarily concerned with compassion he had little option but to be ordained. Today the same man can find ample fulfilment as a probation officer or in one of the welfare services or as a personnel manager in industry. Once all the nurses were nuns. Today they are the glamorous creatures of *Emergency Ward Ten* or amazons who carry banners about pay and conditions.

All these factors are helping to change peoples' lives and thinking. And at the same time, people themselves are in a greater flux than ever. The village blacksmith under his spreading chestnut tree living out his life alongside his village pub and village church, centres of all his social life, has been replaced by the technician who commutes to one town to work and spends the evening in another with the weekend at the local seaside, returning 'home' only late at night to fall into bed after sitting in front of the television. Modern man has so many options and he tries to enjoy them all. The parson (who as a private individual also has all those options) as a parson is left in his parish like the hub of a wheel from which the spokes have disappeared. It can be argued that the neighbourhood would be a lot healthier if it once more developed into a fellowship with some living local reference. But that is not the point. The Church is forever committed to serve men where they are, for it cannot lead them on until it goes and holds their hands in their existing situation.

The surprising thing, as we have said, is that parsons are as widely accepted as the 'persona' of the local community as ever. But accepted for what? It is a question which probably gets more attention from the clergy themselves than from any other section of society. For the one thing which keeps on impressing any parson is his freedom to decide his own priorities. Of course, there are the inescapable diary engagements with their frequent facility for choosing the wrong moments—funerals are a good example. However busy a parson may be he must somehow retain in his diary some flexibility for the unexpected. Then, again, every parson has his own round of parochial chores, not subject to any detailed diary engagements but all requiring to be done by some particular time. But over and above that, the parson has a large proportion of his time which can be assigned at his own discretion. Should he spend an hour whenever it is available in the middle of the afternoon on his knees in prayer? Or at his desk in study? Or more specifically polishing up what he is going to say next Sunday ? Or going the rounds of the local hospital—where he always finds lonely people longing for a chat ? Or should he expose himself to pastoral opportunities by visiting his people's homes—in which case, homes of churchgoers or homes of non-churchgoers ? Or should he just be available in the places where people congregate—to give a personal example: how much time should the Rector of St Bride's, Fleet Street, spend in the Press Club, accessible to any approach ? (In parenthesis; it is sometimes his experience to be accused of dereliction of duty by not being there at some moment when some-one wished he had been.) The point about being a parson is that no one ever asks him to account for how his time is spent nor could anyone, even including his bishop, assess the various items in terms of importance if he told them. It is this, together with a lively sense of stewardship of his time, which leads many parsons to too great an introspection about the nature of their calling and the priority of activities consequent upon it. Like any other sort of introspection, this can become unhealthy, especially when a man is in some isolated parish with few parallel standards with which to compare himself. When we come to talk about bishops we shall see that one of their most vital obligations is to be father to the fathers in God.

One of the most serious of a parson's temptations is to spend too much time wondering exactly how he is called to discharge his particular bit of the ministry—a consideration which sometimes issues in devising impressive formulas or filing systems. They rarely stand up to experience.

It is important to see that the ambiguities of which we have been speaking are inherent in the nature of the ministry. 'To set myself free to the relentless logic of the love of God . . . but . . . never to be scared of leadership' has built right into it a paradox of priorities. While serving God and serving man are ultimately the same service, in the more limited perspectives of this world it can sometimes seem that the service of God in worship can conflict with the service of man—as the characters of the priest and the Levite in the Good Samaritan story show.

This tension between two apparently opposite poles is part of the priestly occupation and there is no escape from it for a full-time employee of the Church. But the burdens of that tension are nowadays being increased by a new adventure into what is the nature of the Church. For many generations, at least, there has been little doubt in the mind of mainstream Christianity, whether catholic or protestant, that a major part of the task was to get people into churches—*extra ecclesiam nulla salus*. Souls had to be plucked like brands from the burning from the *secular* and grafted firmly in the *sacred*. A consequence of the thinking of the last hundred years or so, and not least of the increasing cordiality between religion and science, is that the edges of these two words have been blurred. No longer is the sacred only that which is technically ecclesiastical fastnesses, and the secular the limbo realm of those who have refused incorporation into the Church. It has become increasingly a fundamental of thinking that all the world is God's realm and therefore, as someone has put it, 'there is nothing secular except sin'. The recognition that this is God's world has led to an emphasis on his love for this world. And that inevitably leads to questions about the role of the Church; should it forget its own existence and go out into the world ready to die before it can live? Should the parson be horrified at the mere thought of trying to fill a pew when the pew-occupant could be usefully occupied implementing God's love in an Indian slum or on a factory floor? Does one have to go to church to find God's love or is it there, waiting to be identified, in every corner of his world? Is it true that *laborare est orare* and *orare est laborare*? Such questions have a vital effect on whether the parson spends the unexpected free hour in preparing a sermon or sitting on the local council. But that in turn has implications about his study: should he give his time to theology or is he better occupied reading about the forms of local government and the contents of the latest Government white paper?

This opening up of the Church to the world not only affects each individual parson. It also affects the sources to which he may turn for help and guidance or from which he may expect discipline. For when a Church becomes a pilgrim Church it has little room in its kitbag for intricate trappings of authority. When a pilgrim does not know what is round the next corner he cannot be authoritative about it. All he can do is to have such a background of spiritual experience and standards that he will be able to face whatever turns up and do so in such a way that his actions will commend themselves to others. But this sapping of authority is a serious matter for a Church which has allowed itself to rest too much upon it. Inevitably it raises questions not only like 'Do I have to fast before I receive the Holy Communion?' but also much more fundamental matters such as 'Will you marry me after I have been divorced?' or 'Is there any need for bishops ' Partly, but not wholly, such questions are the result of men having suffered authority revealed in its most hideous authoritarian way by a Hitler or a Stalin and the reaction which ensues. And all this is going on in minds which have been increasingly better educated. The day of the parson as the only scholar in his parish has long gone. He may no longer be even the best theologian (it is astonishing how many people nowadays take theological degrees without getting ordained). The parson whom long tradition had taught to hand out facts and opinions to a passive audience has to learn new modes of participation. The sermon must become something like a dialogue, perhaps by being carried on throughout the week as the parson meets his people. The parson still has a vocation to be a shepherd. But he must no longer treat his people as sheep.

The Church must be in constant process of being re-formed. Never have those words been more true. But, and we repeat this at the risk of tediousness, the significant thing is the way that reform is coming from within the Church. The parson is quicker to recognise the non-ovine character of his flock than the flock themselves. Many parsons in their thinking about lay participation are way ahead of anything the laity themselves can attain at present. The parish as an adult family with every member fully sharing in the decision-making processes as well as in the work is the dream of most parsons. But it would become a nightmare for their parishioners if too rapidly imposed. (It is at this point of lay participation that the Roman Catholic Church has had one of its difficult problems since Vatican II.) The Church in its Councils and in its leaders can propose but the world, whether in or out of the pews, has a ready ability to dispose. The Church, let us never forget for one moment, is as subject to the outside forces of secular structures as Christ was subject to Pilate. But, as John tells us, Christ made the source of that subjection very clear 'Thou couldest have no power at all against me, except it were given thee from above.' The Church is subject to social pressures because it is the extension of the Incarnation, when God subjected himself to human society and all its hazards. The Church's constant questionings of itself and of its ministry is the fruit not of lack of faith but rather of an awareness of the magnitude of Christ and of his sacrifice and of our need to be constantly learning if we are faithfully to follow in his steps. The purpose of God for his Church is as large as the purpose of God worked out in his Christ. We have a long way to go to plumb its depths and know its riches.

The Church, then, and its ministry are *given of God*. While their work will always be in the world, their source and their goal are elsewhere. The Church is God's instrument of salvation and the clergy are its servants. In that sense it remains true that *extra ecclesiam nulla salus* but where we go wrong is in imagining that the Church as we know it has attained the shape that God intends for it. The Church, as we said in another chapter, must be continually in process of becoming and this must equally apply to its ministry. But lest that process of becoming degenerates into a meaningless ramble, we must be ever looking to the source. The Church must be ever pointing away from itself–just as its Lord did–and must be assuring men–by its nature as well as by its words–that baptism into the Church is baptism into Christ and Holy Communion is not only the Church's common meal but also the sharing of the Body and Blood of Christ.

Yet to speak thus is to imply some dichotomy between the Church and Christ and this is to mislead. For the Church has no other head but Christ and – frighteningly – Christ has no other body here on earth. 'Christ has no hands now on earth but yours, no feet but yours, yours are the eyes through which is to look out Christ's compassion on the world' said St Teresa. The function of the Church is to demonstrate the presence of Christ in his work in the world by giving him a body through which to act. It is therefore to be a servant Church and the essence of service is first to find out what the other man needs rather than to do what you think he ought to need. The clergy, then, must spend a great deal of time getting to grips with the world, listening to its voice, feeling its pains.

But the picture does not stop there. 'For the Son of Man came not to be served but to serve, and to give his life a ransom for many' said Mark. That word, ransom, is important. The servant ministry remains inadequate unless it also be a priestly ministry, engaged in offering 'like nature's patient, sleepless Eremite, the moving waters. . . .' George Herbert expressed it in 'Man is the World's High Priest: he doth present the sacrifice for all'.

The minister is called not only down into the depths of the human arena but also into the inner mysteries of the divine presence, entering into the holy of holies to plead before God the offering of God's sacrifice to which he humbly attempts to join his own. Humbly: for anyone who is a priest realises full well how far short he falls. He has always realised it—even *The Thirty-nine Articles* felt constrained to give a whole section to this point, 'On the Unworthiness of Ministers which hinders not the effect of the Sacrament'. Every priest learns early in his ministry to hold to the thought that clean water can flow through a rusty pipe. For this priestly work is one which goes on in spite of sin and failure. It is a service exercised by those who know how desperately they themselves need it. 'I preach'd as never sure to preach again, and as a dying man to dying men,' said Richard Baxter.

No man becomes a priest because he is worthy to be a priest but simply because God calls him. God is in no way dependent on the quality of the material he uses and the Old Testament is the continuing account of how God gave himself through a people which constantly rejected him. On the other hand, it becomes clear that this priestly ministry is something *given*. It is not something which one assumes for oneself. It is therefore something which belongs to specific persons and is given them through a specific formula rather than the spontaneous expression of some personal whim. Anything less than an *ordered* form of ministry cannot be consistent with the standards of a God of order. The New Testament makes it clear that people were chosen by Jesus himself to be leaders and apostles in the Church. Indeed, whenever the Church is mentioned in the New Testament it is always connected with mention of those who were leading it.

Yet it was constantly emphasised that the object of the exercise was that 'we *all* come in the unity of the faith, and of the knowledge of the Son of God, unto a perfect man, unto the measure of the stature of the fulness of Christ' and the measure of that stature always includes his eternal priesthood. Priesthood, in other words, is divinely conferred upon the whole Christian community. All have been received and so all shall offer. The one who is technically called the priest has no more to offer – nor has he a greater duty to offer – than anyone else in the Body. His function is to articulate, to give expression to, the offering and the priesthood of the whole. To give the priest a greater importance than the layman, to regard the layman as a second-class Christian is like suggesting that a man's body exists for the sake of his tongue or maybe his hands. In the Vine all branches are equal. When the world criticises the Church for not doing something, its accusation is as much levelled at the back pew as at the Archbishop of Canterbury. The only difference is that the Archbishop of Canterbury wears a mode of dress which makes him look like a Churchman whereas the tenant of the back pew is more easily disguised. It is essential that the layman remembers this. And equally essential that the Archbishop of Canterbury, and every leader of a Church community however small, never forgets it. For it is the one safeguard against the excessive paternalism which can keep Christians in mental and spiritual swaddling clothes. And the paternalism which can tempt clergy to use the fact of their 'calling' as a big stick to drive the flock into a prison not a fold. Paternalism is a vice. But its opposite pole is also no virtue. The parson who sets out to be 'one of the boys' indistinguishable from the world, let alone the rest of the Church, is not one who is 'never to be scared by leadership'. The heart of the service in which a man is ordained priest is: 'Receive the Holy Ghost for the office and work of a priest in the Church of God, now committed unto thee by the imposition of our hands. Whose sins thou dost forgive, they are forgiven; and whose sins thou dost retain, they are retained. And be thou a faithful dispenser of the Word of God, and of his holy Sacraments . . .' And a moment later: 'Take thou authority. . .' The priest is forever called to conform to Christ, not to the ways of the world and he never more sadly injures men than when he fails them at this level. Whether he be national Church leader or a new curate at a youth club session which can go awry, the duty of discernment and guidance is laid upon him. The best of all servants is the one who refuses to do a disservice to his master even though that master order it. His friends longed for Christ to set up the kingdom of Israel – as they understood it – immediately. He refused. The Christian servant must also know when to refuse.

In all things, Christ is to be the sole pattern of the minister. The very essence of Christ is that he, who was and is all perfection, became enfleshed in contemporary man. Even though he is the epitome of man and therefore of all men of all ages, he nevertheless became in his Incarnation strictly contemporary man of the period o A.D. Had God delayed the Incarnation until now and let it be in western Europe, the Christ would not have appeared quite the same. He would not have worn the costume of two thousand years ago, he would not have used the language of a rustic people. In other words, the accidents of the Incarnation would have been different. But its substance, the relation of Christ to God the Father and to all men and his saving work, would have remained the same. It is that relation which is the heart of the given-ness of the Incarnation. And it is that relation which is the heart of the given-ness of the work of the minister. The substance of the ministry, then, is the God-man relationship. But its accidents are those of its generation. To see what the ministry is, one looks at

God, to see how it works in any age, one looks at the world. The nature of the ministry, being derived from God, remains unalterable. The exercise of the ministry, being a service to the world, must not follow the same form from age to age. This raises a question which many feel should have been aired quite a long time ago: is the present form of the ministry of the Church of England the right one? And behind that lies the deeper question: in days of the open, pluralist society is there any need of a specific group of men set apart as ministers after some ceremony of ordination?

With few exceptions, the whole of Christendom accepts that by baptism a man enters into the ministry of the Church and becomes 'Christ's faithful soldier and servant'. The Church of England, in tune with the majority of Christendom, believes that something further is added by ordination. The very use of words like 'something further' leads us into difficulties for it suggests that something is missing from the ordination which is baptism. And it can very easily lead to that sad distortion which suggests that a priest is a baptised person with some magical plus-factor which makes him a channel of grace. There is, quite certainly, nothing magical about it for magic means being able to control God by using the right occult phrases and actions. And a priest exists to serve God, not to turn on some powerful tap which releases his mercies after the right fee or formula.

The priest is not a magician. But, on the other hand, he is something more than a man who goes through a ceremony in order to spend his full time as a parish organiser or a diocesan administrator. The Church, like any human organisation, needs organisers and officers to perform certain functions on her behalf but such things can be equally well done by laymen. You don't have to be ordained to get a new tile put on the church roof.

The priest is a man who has heard an inward call to a certain set of duties in the Church and whose inward call has been answered by an outward call from the Church itself to do those duties. In order to embark upon those duties he makes solemn vows from which he expects no release in this life. The beginning of those

duties is when God acting through this Church which acts through
its representative, the bishop, commissions the man to do them.
This commission has come down from Christ himself who handed
it to the first apostles who handed it to their successors and so on.
Which need not imply any unbroken pipeline from one bishop's
hands to another down the centuries for that, too, has elements of
magic about it. Rather it implies that since Christ inaugurated his
Church, that Church has gone on, through many vicissitudes and
under varying guises maybe, but gone on nevertheless. This continuity is established not by human efforts to preserve the life-
stream but by Christ's own promise, that even the gates of hell
should not prevail against it. Nevertheless, this continuity has had
a human form and it has taken the shape of bishops, priests and
deacons.

In the natural order, species have developed certain organs and
where they have proved useful have retained them and where they
have proved unhelpful have let them atrophy. A similar process
has gone on in the Church. The New Testament cannot be described as explicitly setting out the threefold ministry. But under
the guidance of the Holy Spirit the Church has developed varying
forms and those which have proved useful and meaningful have
survived. The Church did not organise itself according to any
academic discussion nor yet as a result of high theological expertise.
Rather in that Pentecostal outburst of its early life one finds many
forms and feels even more. But gradually the threefold ministry
becomes the significant pattern.

We cannot, then, turn to Scripture as the final authority to tell
us exactly what happens when a man gets ordained. Nor does early
Church history record struggles and debates and decisions on this
topic. Always in primitive Christianity the emphasis is on the
Body of Christ as a whole, each member having his own functions
but each inalienably dependent on the whole. To suggest, therefore,
that the priest is in any way a mediator cannot be right, for a
mediator stands outside the body on behalf of which he mediates.
That would mean three entities, God, men and mediators. There
are only two poles. God and man and always and again one has to

return to this metaphor of the Body. To quote Bishop Gore:[1] 'It is an abuse of the sacerdotal conception, if it is supposed that the priesthood exists to celebrate sacrifices or acts of worship in the place of the body of people or as their substitute. . . . The ministry is no more one of vicarious action than it is one of exclusive knowledge or exclusive spiritual relation to God. What is the truth then? It is that the Church is one body. The free approach to God in the Sonship and Priesthood of Christ belongs to men as members of "one body", and this one body has different organs through which the functions of its life find expression, as it was differentiated by the act and appointment of him who created it. The reception, for instance, of Eucharistic grace, the approach to God in Eucharistic sacrifice, are functions of the whole body. "*We* bless the cup of blessing." "*We* break the bread", says Paul, speaking for the community; "*We* offer", "*We* present" is the language of the liturgies. But the ministry is the organ – the necessary organ – of these functions. It is the hand which offers and distributes; it is the voice which consecrates and pleads. And the whole body can no more dispense with its services than the natural body can grasp or speak without the instrumentality of hand or tongue. Thus the ministry is the instrument as well as the symbol of the Church's unity, and no man can share her fellowship except in acceptance of its office.'

What is conferred in ordination, then, is a status, inherently involving capacities, duties, responsibilities. It does not confer a deeper relationship with God or an obligation to a higher standard of holiness or a more ready access to divine wisdom. There is no spiritual caste system in the Body of Christ. The priest cannot perform God's service in the layman's stead nor can he propitiate God on the layman's behalf. The layman who 'leaves it to the parson' misunderstands both the parson's calling and his own and he is arguing from spiritual indolence rather than theological knowledge. In the Church spiritual endowments are offered equally to clergy and laity. The difference is that to the layman they are personal whereas to the priest they are corporate (in his office as

[1] *The Church and the Ministry*, pp. 85–6.

priest: he is also, as still being in his person a layman, offered them personally). What has caused much confusion is the change which has happened in the connotation of the word 'lay'. To us it means someone who is a 'not'. To the doctor a layman is one who knows little about medicine, to a lawyer, one who knows little of the law. But in the Church the only meaning the word can rightly have is derived from its origins. In the Bible the *laos* means the whole People of God. It is a word of positive meaning and spiritual privilege.

Perhaps the most helpful way of summing up the difference between priest and layman is by quoting *Ordained Ministry Today*,[1] a small but quite invaluable report of the Ministry Committee of the Church Assembly's Advisory Council for the Church's Ministry: 'The analogy of love and marriage is helpful. A married man is different in so far as he has new obligations, new responsibilities. In fulfilling these he shows the nature of marriage. Yet marriage is more than just providing house-keeping, being at home and giving the occasional bunch of flowers. It is more than doing all the right things. We know what the signs and acts of love are, but by themselves they are not love. Yet love is empty without them. They disclose love. So the priesthood is disclosed through those characteristic acts which belong to the ministry of Christ, and to the equipping of all God's people for that ministry; communicating the faith, caring pastorally for people, and exercising leadership and presidency, especially in worship and sacrament. That is to say, it is these characteristic acts interpreted in terms of God's purposes for the church and the world. It is the heart of ordination that it sets a man to stand for the given-ness of God by doing them. Nothing less than this, and nothing more, is implied by ordination.'

The analogy in that quotation can be pursued one stage further. The essence of marriage is that two people make solemn vows to each other and God accepts those vows and creates out of them a particular new body with specific functions attached to it. They are functions to be exercised on God's behalf–for children are to be 'brought up in the fear and nurture of his holy name' and also

[1] Church Information Office, 1969.

on behalf of society–for all who come into contact with children thus brought up should benefit by it. We believe that the ceremony of Holy Matrimony confers a special grace for the fulfilment of those vows but that it has no magical character guaranteeing the maintenance of those vows or contracting God to force them to come true is obvious. One more point, while the marriage service confers upon two people a distinctive new *persona* as man and wife and gives them entrée to their own privileges and intimacies, it does not in any way set them apart from the world. Rather, since they have entered the status through which procreation is blessed, they have more fully entered into both the heritage and the future of mankind.

The priesthood, then, is the authority conferred by God to perform certain functions. But it is none the less also conferred by the men and women who make up the Church. While the priest is always dependent upon God for the power of his ministry he is no less dependent on man for its authority. Thus is a priest always both open to the grace of God and subject to the social pressures which exist in the church in his day or in his area. Such pressures can be inhibiting, for all institutions have their own built-in con-servatisms. Such can be a source of exasperation but there is nothing to do about it except not 'be scared of leadership'. Mean-while every priest finds himself in some ways a captive of the status his flock confer upon him. A personal example will illustrate. I had been able to help a starving family until some sick pay came through. The moment that money arrived the mother sent out–most unsuitably–for some sticky cakes. As I happened to be in the house when they arrived, the mother insisted that I ate one before the children were allowed so much as a nibble. The status of the parson had to be respected. I am not certain whether the sensation of food sticking in my throat or big brown hungry eyes watching me is the more vivid part of that memory. But the mother was satisfied that the status of the parson, as she saw it, was preserved.

The intrusion of so personal an anecdote will perhaps hint at the difficulty of writing this chapter where in a sense I have had to put myself under a microscope and produce autobiographical records of what I see. Fortunately, this section can soon end. But there is one area which must be touched upon before it does.

It is to point out that all the foregoing, personal though it may be, consists of generalisations. The particularities of each individual priest's sphere of work are the grounds of an infinite diversity. The priest in the dormitory village, empty all day as his flock commute to the city, has problems and opportunities quite different from those of the priest in the city whose parish dies at 5 p.m. of an evening and is the resort at weekends only of tourists and tramps. The man who works in a new housing estate has in many ways to exercise a different priesthood from the one who has spent half a lifetime in a secluded but mature rural community which has its own personality – and, usually, its own prejudices – and the vicar of a mining village needs different approaches from his brother in a university town. And the working days of chaplains, hospital, school, embassy, forces, prison and so on, are different again.

Yet to all of them is committed the same charge; to preach the word, to exercise the compassion of Christ and to minister the Sacraments. From age to age the Church has adjudged their relative importance differently but there can be no valid distinction. Each has its vital part to play and each merges into the others. To all priests, in one degree or another, is committed the duty of proclaiming God's Word. Some will do so more readily by traditional sermon or by personal conversation, others will develop a facility for print and the electronic media. Whatever his channel, there will remain for every priest the same need not only to have studied theology in some perhaps far distant seminary days but also to keep up with it. For theology, no less than any other mental pursuit, finds new material and argues new theories and reaches new conclusions. The priest who diligently gives himself to the ministry of the Word finds he has a full-time job.

Then there is the pastoral care which is compassion. It is the area in which he meets personal needs and anxieties. And again, there is no small amount of assimilation needed. For to advise an old age pensioner involves knowing the latest rulings of the

Ministry while a tramp at the door can call for familiarity with social security laws and their local offices. The divine love must be proclaimed in deed as well as in word. And again, to do that adequately can take all the time a priest can find.

But neither of these parts of his ministry can be allowed to happen at the expense of the ministry of the Sacraments along with which go the 'occasional offices'–marriages, funerals and the like. The following of the rites of the Sacraments requires little expertise. It is all there on paper. But is it? Can the Sacraments be faithfully approached except from a background of prayer and meditation? Here are the effective signs of the presence and action of God. You cannot be casual about that. Nor can you be casual about the appurtenances which have grown up around the Sacraments; the choice of hymns, for example, cannot be made by sticking a pin in the book. Then again, the man who is to officiate at a marriage without spending much time with bride and bridegroom is depriving two young people of something to which they have the right: to be made aware of God's interest in their excitement, the implications of the fact that Jesus did his first miracle at a village girl's wedding in Cana. And once more, we have found a full-time occupation for a priest.

All of which means three full-time occupations at least. Manifestly impossible. So back he goes to his ancient question of priorities. But always with the comfort of knowing that whichever he does it is indeed God's work. And also the comfort of knowing that he works not on his own but with the backing and support of the whole of his flock. For each of the ministries outlined above is also laid, to a greater or lesser degree, upon each baptised person. And alongside that goes what must be the increasing practice of the Church, to organise group ministries where a man may exercise all the facets of his priesthood but give the maximum time to that part for which he has the best natural gifts.

Such group ministries can be only one part of the experimentation to which the Church is urgently called at this moment. History forces us to the conclusion that such trial and error is likely to be too little and too late rather than–what would be more characteristic of the early Christians—daring and reliant on the Holy Spirit. But the Church which, as we have insisted, is inevitably influenced by the society it serves, cannot remain static in days of such universal revolution. The days when a man's theological training, completed before he was twenty-three years old, could be expected to serve adequately for half a century, have gone and so have the days when the clergy were largely drawn from one particular part of society. What was perhaps inevitable when education was expensive is undesirable when it is universally available. But even the question of the education of a priest must be re-examined radically. Is there any longer an advantage for all in a close acquaintance with Greek verbs? And then there is the other very major question: does a priest any longer have to give his whole time to his priesthood or shall we see increasing numbers of 'tentmakers' who make their living in some 'secular' job but devote their spare time to the ministry? And where in all this will women fit in? We seem to have reached the stage where there is growing recognition that there is no very visible reason against their ordination and every reason for—except the factor which has played so large a part in Church history, 'we have never done it that way'. Perhaps to dismiss that factor casually is wrong. But to give it undue importance might be even more wrong.

*   *   *

This chapter has reached the point of discussing matters which are on the periphery, in practical if not emotional terms. Yet it has thus far deliberately avoided talking of the most talked-about of all ecclesiastical offices: the bishop.

There are two reasons for this: and, superficially, they seem contradictory.

1. A bishop always remains a priest. Therefore everything already said about priests remains true of him. Hence it seemed good to get those points established first.

2. A bishop is different from a priest though many of the differences are only a matter of degree.

Most people do not spend a lot of time consorting with bishops and therefore get little chance of knowing them. It is little wonder if, like medieval cartographers who had reached the limits of their knowledge, they inscribe on the *terra incognita* 'Here be dragons'. Not a few bishops in the past, at least, have acted in such a way as to support the theory that they are proud pompous, prelatical monsters who eventually turn out to be mythical. Occasionally they are still given to the eccentric dress which recalls a dash of the Tudor court, the needs of an equestrian as far as their legs are concerned, the awe of patrician purple, puzzling pieces of jewellery, all encapsulated in a rich-acred medieval palace, to which the plebs approach humbly murmuring 'Your Lordship' and there comes a patronising reply in the mystical language known as episcopalese.

One of the more lively moments of the last Lambeth Conference occurred when one bishop proposed that all honorifics, peculiar dress, and so on should be abandoned. One contributor to the debate made a poignant remark. On becoming a bishop he had determined to avoid aprons and breeches – if only on grounds of expense. One day he received an invitation to Speech Day at a school, 'And,' said the headmaster, 'please dress as a bishop *for the sake of the boys.*'

There are many bishops who would live much less cluttered lives *if only the laity would let them.* Perhaps it is the memory of days when bishops were great officers of State with all the consequent patronage which causes laymen thus to falsify their position. Or perhaps it's a conviction that if you can make him unreal in appearance you can neutralise the demands of what he stands for. Whatever the reason, much of the image of bishops is largely what the laity have made it, not the bishops themselves.

But there are also illusions within the Church itself. Bishop Stephen Bayne has given colourful words to some of them: 'We [the bishops] have been thought of at times as what I can only call the Queen Bees of the Church, in luxurious captivity, with plethoric and disturbed abdomens, surrounded by busy, buzzing presbyters fanning us with their wings and feeding us with the purest honey, in order solely that we may lay our ecclesiastical eggs in ordination and confirmation, in abundant supply, for the perpetuation of the hive.'[1]

To isolate ordination and confirmation is to give these acts some strange magical significance. To see perpetuation as an end in itself is to parody a Church which must be ready to die unto itself.

We had better try to get on firm ground. What does the Church officially say about bishops? By and large it might be said that Anglicanism is reluctant to define the nature of episcopacy but it unequivocally insists on retaining it. But there is one safe source we can look to. Here are two sentences from the Preface to the Ordinal: 'It is evident unto all men diligently reading Holy Scripture and ancient Authors, that from the Apostles' time there have been these Orders of Ministers in Christ's Church; Bishops, Priests and Deacons. . . . No man shall be accounted or taken to be a lawful Bishop, Priest or Deacon in the Church of England or suffered to execute any of the said functions, except he be called, tried, examined and admitted thereto. . . .'

'From the Apostles' time there have been . . .' Historically there is little question that episcopacy has been regarded as the fulness of the Church's ministry from the earliest times and throughout the overwhelming majority of the Church. But this must not be distorted into some mechanical pipeline theory of a successive transmission of power: for that, too is magical. The office of a bishop is apostolic by its nature, not by virtue of some unbroken contact with Christ's first ministers. The Church has retained episcopacy because, just as any living organism acquires and retains useful organs, it has found it useful. But even though the mechanical pipeline view is untenable, we must never lose sight of the fact that a bishop is pre-eminently a link, between past and future, between one place and another, and so on.

1. The Church has found episcopacy useful as the principal organ of continuity. An annually elected Moderator may be a better man than some bishops. But he has a much lesser chance of reminding his flock of past glories and vicissitudes.

2. The bishop is the principal organ of the Church's unity. As

[1] *Living Church* (U.S.A.), 9th December 1962.

this book has struggled to say, the Church of England, quite properly, includes a wide diversity of thought. The true bishop is the personal symbol of the common life which underlies it all. There is deep meaning in the fact that it is only to a bishop that the Book of Common Prayer accords the title 'Father-in-God' (which emphasises both the characteristics of a father and also their Source). The striking thing is how many men who have histories as partisans become, after their consecration, true Fathers-in-God even to those who were once their opponents.

3. The bishop is the Church's principal liturgical officer. The traditional glory of the English cathedrals for their standards of worship stems from their relationship with the man above all charged to maintain those standards.

4. The bishop is the chief guardian of orthodoxy and also its chief teacher though never must he assume that he defines orthodoxy by any personal judgement. He speaks for the Church as a whole.

5. The bishop is the chief minister. All too often this has been distorted to make him the chief administrator. Administration is an inevitable part of a bishop's task and it is indeed a part of his ministry in the name of Christ. But it must not absorb the whole.

6. He is the spearhead of the Church's mission. He himself is sent and he sends others.

The bishop is all those things in his own diocese. But it is vital that they are seen in the context of the second sentence from the Ordinal quoted above. 'Except he be called.'

(a) A bishop must be called of God. For until he is called he cannot be sent. And 'apostle' and 'missionary' are no more than the Greek and Latin form of that word.

(b) A bishop must be called by the Church. The burden of history, devolving nomination on to the Prime Minister, has obscured that fact for us but it nevertheless remains true that no man becomes a bishop until the Church translates a letter from 10 Downing Street into a request from itself and its own actions consequent upon it.

The essence of this lies in the word 'admitted'. After a man has been tried and examined he still has to be brought into the episcopal status. He has to be consecrated. This does not mean he is suddenly given some new sagacity (though it is interesting in episcopal biographies to see how frequently this does actually follow), nor that he is given control of some new sacramental power (for all power is, and remains, God's). The Consecration of bishops is the outward form of acceptance that a man has been called of God and the Church to exercise episcopal functions and a statement on his part of his acceptance of that call and his determination to honour it. But, even more, this ceremony is an appeal to God to grant that man all that is necessary for his calling. For unless God has called him and continually equips him, all else is vain.

So the bishop goes forward to his diocese. He must remember that being a servant of the apostolic Christ he is sent to all the people of that diocese, not only those who carry membership cards. Being a servant of the pastoral Christ, he must be father to all men and especially to the clergy, for they have nowhere else to turn. Being a servant of the eternal Christ, he must remember he is a link between past and future. Being a servant of the universal Christ, he must link the slums at one end of his diocese with the wealth at the other, the peasant and the prince. And, in Church of England terms, the high and the low, the Catholic and the Protestant.

The bishop, even when cleansed of the caricatures which historical accident has cluttered about him, needs abundant grace to fulfil his high calling. Anglicans believe that God is aware of this and takes the necessary steps. There are, it is true, cases where God proposes and man disposes and a bishop falls down on his job. But they are rare and point the truth that perfection is never a property of human affairs, even when they are directed towards the divine.

6

The Balance Sheet

Land values in the City of London are among the highest in the world. One of the biggest plots of land in the City is occupied by St Paul's Cathedral. There are 17,755 parochial churches and chapels in England. Many of them are on prominent sites worth a fortune to a property developer. Add to that the treasures of craftsmanship in those churches and chapels at today's prices in the open market. We need not continue to list the glebe land, endowments, parsons' houses and the rest of the acquisitions of centuries.

The Church of England, on the surface at least, appears to be very wealthy. It is little wonder that a very vocal ginger group within the Church clamours for all this wealth to be realised (just like Egypt is selling bits of pyramids and royal tombs) and the proceeds to be given to the world's poor.

Sell the jewelled chalices, they say, brushing aside the fact that they were given as a sacred trust which cannot lightly be dismissed. Knock down St Paul's say the extremists, and let worship once more be in a plain upper room. The argument that a building can in itself be an act of worship does not move them. That, quite apart from any sacred function, it is a part of English culture and the world's aesthetic heritage does not matter to them.

The moment that God became incarnate in Jesus Christ, someone had to provide somewhere for him to lay his head, if only a manger. And somebody had to pay the grocer's bill. The Church, his Body, incarnate in the world, inevitably has to have physical necessities like buildings while its officers have to pay bills like anyone else. But has it all got out of proportion?

The deep moral questions hidden in that are complex indeed. But at least we can get at the facts. What is the financial structure of the Church of England?

Best known, but usually least understood, of all the Church of England financial agencies are the Church Commissioners. It is as well to dispose of an ancient canard immediately. They do not operate, or own, any slum property nor do they run brothels in Paddington or anywhere else. That is a story which persisted (it is now surely dead) by virtue of its colourfulness rather than any semblance of truth.

The Church Commissioners are now just over twenty years old. In that time they have increased their income to nearly three times the 1948 figure. That is good management by any standards. But it is not ruthless. They avoid investments in things like breweries and companies who specialise in armament production as well as several other categories. The Commissioners' main job is to manage funds which are largely derived from the ancient endowments of the Church, whether in money, real estate or whatever, and to apply the results to improving the living conditions of the clergy of the Church of England. They also administer other work for the Church under statutory authority. They get nothing from the State, though they are a statutory body.

Because of their devotion and expertise the minimum stipend for a beneficed clergyman, which stood at £350 a year in 1948, now very rarely falls below £1,000 while assistant curates, that is to say, diocesan clergy who are not incumbents or dignitaries now average more than £800 a year including family allowances. The Commissioners have also done a great deal to improve the housing of the clergy and the ancient image of a twenty-nine bedroom rectory vulnerable to every draught under heaven and killing a lonely parson's wife with a scrubbing brush is now largely a thing of the past. The Commissioners also now own and maintain all the diocesan bishops' houses, having acquired the episcopal endowments at the same time as they took over the properties. Another important improvement they have made is in clergy pensions – in 1948 £200 a year, now a basic £650 plus a £1,000 lump sum on retirement (which is very necessary for a man whose retirement means vacating the house he lives in). Since 1954 the Commissioners have also been empowered to help church building in new development areas – they have assisted some 1,100 mission ventures.

And, for those who like pondering ecclesiastical bureaucracy, they have done something which surely deserves trumpets. They have increased their work enormously and at the same time reduced their staff complement.

The Commissioners, across the road from the House of Lords, have done wonders. Even so, their present income meets little more than one third of the total expenditure of the Church of England. In 1968 their total income was £21,889,356. Set against that the total number of clergy 18,256, excluding those who have retired. The arithmetic shows there is no vast surplus of wealth in the Commissioners' coffers.

The Commissioners' powers and duties are derived from Parliament by a series of Acts of Parliament and Measures of the Church Assembly. The Commissioners are required by statute to send copies of their Annual Report and Accounts to Parliament and Questions on their work can be asked in Parliament. The Commissioners are similarly required to send copies of their Report and Accounts to the Church Assembly where they are also open to Questions. The Central Board of Finance has no direct connection with Parliament. It exists 'to serve as the financial executive body of the Church of England'. It deals more with current funds as against the Commissioners mainly endowments. It has roughly the same degree of popularity as does the Chancellor of the Exchequer in the eyes of a tax payer and for the same reasons. It derives its resources, which in 1969 exceeded £1 million, mainly from diocesan quotas which in turn come from parochial quotas which, by and large, means the collection plate. The Central Board of Finance is answerable to the Church Assembly. Roughly a quarter of its income goes on training candidates for the ministry while another £50,000 or so goes to pensions for full time layworkers and clergy widows. The rest is applied to centralised activities such as the Church Information Office, the Board for Social Responsibility, the Board of Education, the Missionary and Ecumenical Council, central administration, and so on. It is only the agent of the direct grants made by the Church of England to the British Council of

Churches, the Lambeth Conference, the Anglican Centre in Rome and comparable activities. The Central Board also runs an investment office on behalf of trustees of charitable funds connected with the Church of England. It has an impressive record of achievement.

Behind the Central Board of Finance stand the Boards of Finance set up by each diocese. Like the Central Board, they estimate their needs in advance, collect the resources by a quota system and disburse them through the various official bodies.

From this merest glimpse of official funds we turn to the voluntary organisations, many of which by long and honourable history have become official in all but the fact that they are not subject to central Church authority. The *Church of England Year Book* lists a couple of hundred of them. They include such bodies as the Missionary Societies, the Mothers Union, the Actors Church Union, the Samaritans Incorporated, the Plainsong and Medieval Music Society, the Church of England Children's Society and so on. One gets the impression that at some time someone has founded a Church organisation to meet every conceivable human need and every divine aspiration. Between them they administer vast funds, almost invariably with a striking blend of devotion and acumen.

These voluntary organisations are in some ways the best example of much of what this book has been trying to say. The primary characteristic of the Church of England is its desire to treat people as responsible adults. It does not seek to set up a set of detailed theological statements accompanied by an equally detailed code of behaviour. Instead it says, this is what the Christian faith is about, make your response to it in your own way as an individual, remembering always that your very individuality depends on your relationship with the whole and the health of the whole. Such words are addressed to its clergy no less than to its laity. The consequence is that each feels free to achieve fulfilment by developing his own gifts alongside carrying out his own routine duties. Thus a Tubby Clayton will see in Flanders mud the germ of a men's fellowship and Toc H is born or a Chad Varah will be filled with compassion for the suicidal and create Samaritans or a Thomas Bray will see sheep without a shepherd in the New World and as a consequence the Society for Promoting Christian Knowledge and the Society for the Propagation of the Gospel begin centuries of service. Sometimes the conception of these works matches their moment of opportunity and a great organisation springs up, perhaps to the surprise of its founding father. More often a village Hampden is a better image and a man does great things in his own backyard, in no way diminished because they fail to catch the eye of a reporter. The apologist, of course, regrets this fact because it means the long tables of statistics he would like to quote are simply not available. Nor does the historian find his task easy when confronted with the problem of assessing an untidy picture of infinitely diverse talents finding infinitely diverse expression. But life itself is not tidy. There is no neat way of deciding where it shall bubble up next. High power conferences and committees draw up their blue-prints. Then the Spirit alights on some simple country rectory and a mighty movement ensues. The Church of England has about it an unpredictability which is the despair of a bureaucrat. It is the Church of a poet, not of a computer. It is easier to live with a series of transistors which will yield only what is programmed into them. The computer does not speak until you press its button. The murmur of the Spirit who brooded over the face of the waters as Chaos became Cosmos has continued down all the centuries. But his mark is unpredictability.

In an age like ours, so inured to planning and productivity assessment, this is a hard saying. People conditioned to blue-prints are likely to be bewildered by a Church which responds to a sudden inspiration. The Church is inevitably tempted to follow the planner. Committed, as it is, to be immersed in society, it can get too obsessed by 'strategy'. And, like an innkeeper in Bethlehem, it can have all its rooms allocated when the great visitor arrives. We are right to agonise over empty, decaying churches, ill adapted to present needs. We are right to protest when the twentieth-century Church gets lost in nineteenth-century nostalgia. We are right about so many of the criticisms made inside the Church and beyond its walls. But let us never presume that human planning is all that is needed. The Church has, Janus-like, to face two ways.

Its eyes must be on God and man and it must always seek to discern ways of serving both. Service—ministry—is its keynote.

In a presidential address to the Convocation of Canterbury Dr Michael Ramsey expressed it well. He had been talking of the emphasis on the Church as servant. He had made the point that the New Testament has two words for servant, 'diaconos' and 'doulos'. 'The word deacon', he said, 'means to be performing certain actions towards other people in looking after them and their needs. It is a functional word. Christ came to be a deacon. . . . But the word doulos (slave) is different. It tells not of a man's activities but of his relation to his owner. The slave is a man who belongs to another, with no rights, no status, totally bound and obliged to the one to whom he belongs. The apostles were Christ's slaves, and Christ himself was obedient to the Father as God's slave, absorbed in the Father's will. If the Servant Church is going to be our theme . . . let us be sure what we are saying. We are saying that Christian people are here to be like deacons, attending to every human need which Christian imagination can see and respond to. But we are also saying that Christians are here as men and women who are owned by God, who belong not to themselves but totally to him, who have no rights against him, who are ready to have his majesty and glory as their ceaseless priority, and who are not ashamed to tell a freedom-loving world that there is a bondage of obedience wherein true freedom may be found.'

The Church of England is certainly a deacon Church, serving in an impressive diversity of ways—some of them appearing to the outsider to topple from serving into obsequious lackeydom, but the Church of England is also right at its very heart (which makes its heart right) a doulos Church. Its very vulnerability to criticism is part of that emptying which, as Paul told the Philippians, the Christ endured when he became obedient unto death, even the death of the Cross. Wherefore God hath highly exalted him. Spiritual exaltation is not yet the characteristic of the Church of England. But at least, God has thought enough of it to keep it in being throughout the centuries in spite of all its shortcomings.

But will all this continue? Is the Church still 'militant here on earth' or has it become dormant?

It cannot be too often said that the Church is a divine institution whose raw material is humans. Those humans are in this as in every other activity subject to the cycle of day and night, optimism and depression. We have been passing through one of the darker cycles. Morale has fallen low. But that is a remark which applies to society as a whole. Exuberance is not the mark of our politics, our economies, our arts at the present time. And even the thrills of our triumphant science are both shortlived and laced with pessimism. We reach the moon and frighten ourselves at the thought of it as a military base. We probe the threshold of life and shudder at the thought of test-tube babies. We heal the sick and produce the problems of geriatrics. Despite all our material assurances we have become a worried generation. The foundations are rumbling. There is nothing new in this. It has always been an insecure world but somehow the nineteenth century concealed this from the West. We have once more come face to face with facts.

Human morale is not at present buoyant and this casts its shadows into the Church. Yet a straight look at the facts shows the Church as more vigorous than its social context.

The baptised membership of the Church of England is some fifty per cent of the population. That is a far higher percentage than votes for any political party at a general election. Add in membership of other Churches and you have a far greater number of people in England saying Yes to Christianity than there are casting any sort of vote at an election. It is much more time-consuming to make arrangements with a parson, fix up godparents and get to church on time for a baptism than it is to push a piece of paper into a ballot box.

There is little doubt that many parents have only vestigial traces of Christianity when they bring their babies to the font. But quite certainly the act can never be construed as the rejection of Christ which is implied when people carelessly use phrases like 'pagan' or 'post-christian' England. But, says the critic, look now many of those baptised children fail to come to Confirmation. Well, the number of confirmed is about 9,500,000. More than the total membership of the Trade Union Congress. Or again, we lament over vast churches with sparse congregations. But let the local M.P. address a meeting. He will get a still smaller number. And add those congregations together, even on a wet English Sunday, and you have a larger total than the country can show for any activity other than entertainment—which for most people is a passivity, not an activity.

The truth is that more people in England are interested in Christianity than in politics. The *Humanae Vitae* Encyclical storm has raged far more fiercely than any political issue. Taken in the absolute there is little comfort in that statement. But it does point to the fact that any malaise is not the affliction solely of the Church. The Church of England remains the largest institution in this country and it will have to decline a lot further before that statement loses its truth. The amount of space given to Christianity in our newspapers and the number of religious books sold does not imply the lack of public interest which would lead to such a decline.

We must not blink the truth; all is far from well in the Church. But it is time that so many church people ceased acting as if they believed that the Christian virtue of humility reached its optimum when it becomes a diabolical masochism of self-denigration. The New Testament character who buried his talent did not gain the Lord's approval.

The Church is the biggest institution in this country. But even more important than that, it is the most *personal*. Even if the local parson does happen to be a diffident and somewhat unapproachable type, he is *there*, in every village, and his house is readily identifiable. Furthermore, he lives and acts as a person, not as the local antenna of a remote bureaucracy. And he has found that all the great ideas he collected from his seminary or dimly heard about from Church House, Westminster, do not help until he learns to treat people as people. Bureaucracy can hide itself behind a form filled in triplicate. The parson is there, on the spot, vulnerable.

That very vulnerability helps to make him acceptable. It was when God made himself vulnerable that the Christian Faith began. To the Greeks it was foolishness. But God chose what the world counted folly to confound what the world counted wise.

The Church is a beacon down the centuries. It is also, to use Rose Macaulay's phrase 'all the dark unchristened deeds of christened men'. The Church must always be acutely conscious of belonging to the world. It must also always be proclaiming that the Kingdoms of the world are to become the Kingdom of God. The Church is eternal, a reflection of the unchanging God. At the same time constantly *in via*, on the way, for the Spirit has much leading to do before it attains all truth. The Church is a city set on a hill, there for all to see. At the same time the Church is salt, which can do its hidden work only when deep inside the situation. It is the seed sown in darkness to blossom in the light. The Church is where the paradox of God the Creator, Lord of all things, and God the Redeemer, staggering beneath a cross, is made visible. The Church is God's eternal answer. But to do its work it must become part of the problem. The Church is where the paradox of man, formed of the dust, destined for glory, is finally resolved.

John Updike noticed in London 'an odd number of steeples with their tops cut off, like daggers made safe for children to play with'. His picturesque phrase means more than he might have thought. For God has contained his glory within the compass of man's comprehension. He has processed his strong meat and made it fit for babes. And the Church founded upon the rock of Jesus Christ is its earthly and earthy channel.

The Church of England is part of all that. And since this is a personal book, I allow myself a personal conclusion. I rejoice in it in the name of the Lord.

Index

INDEX